Y0-BRR-804

Question Framing and Response Consistency

Robin M. Hogarth, *Editor*

**NEW DIRECTIONS FOR METHODOLOGY OF
SOCIAL AND BEHAVIORAL SCIENCE**

DONALD W. FISKE, *Editor-in-Chief*

Number 11, March 1982

Paperback sourcebooks in
The Jossey-Bass Social and Behavioral Sciences Series

Jossey-Bass Inc., Publishers
San Francisco • Washington • London

H
61
.Q3
1982

Question Framing and Response Consistency
Number 11, March 1982
        Robin M. Hogarth, *Editor*

New Directions for Methodology of Social and Behavioral Science Series
Donald W. Fiske, *Editor-in-Chief*

Copyright © 1982 by Jossey-Bass Inc., Publishers
                        and
                        Jossey-Bass Limited

Copyright under International, Pan American, and Universal
Copyright Conventions. All rights reserved. No part of
this issue may be reproduced in any form — except for brief
quotation (not to exceed 500 words) in a review or professional
work — without permission in writing from the publishers.

New Directions for Methodology of Social and Behavioral Science
is published quarterly by Jossey-Bass Inc., Publishers.
Subscriptions, single-issue orders, change of address notices,
undelivered copies, and other correspondence should be sent to
New Directions Subscriptions, Jossey-Bass Inc., Publishers,
433 California Street, San Francisco, California 94104.

Editorial correspondence should be sent to the Editor-in-Chief,
Donald W. Fiske, University of Chicago, Chicago, Illinois 60637.

Library of Congress Catalogue Card Number LC 81-48486
International Standard Serial Number ISSN 0271-1249
International Standard Book Number ISBN 87589-911-0

Cover art by Willi Baum
Manufactured in the United States of America

Ordering Information

The paperback sourcebooks listed below are published quarterly and can be ordered either by subscription or as single copies.

Subscriptions cost $35.00 per year for institutions, agencies, and libraries. Individuals can subscribe at the special rate of $21.00 per year *if payment is by personal check.* (Note that the full rate of $35.00 applies if payment is by institutional check, even if the subscription is designated for an individual.) Standing orders are accepted.

Single copies are available at $7.95 when payment accompanies order, and *all single-copy orders under $25.00 must include payment.* (California, Washington, D.C., New Jersey, and New York residents please include appropriate sales tax.) For billed orders, cost per copy is $7.95 plus postage and handling. (Prices subject to change without notice.)

To ensure correct and prompt delivery, all orders must give either the *name of an individual* or an *official purchase order number.* Please submit your order as follows:

Subscriptions: specify series and subscription year.
Single Copies: specify sourcebook code and issue number (such as, MSBS8).

Mail orders for United States and Possessions, Latin America, Canada, Japan, Australia, and New Zealand to:
Jossey-Bass Inc., Publishers
433 California Street
San Francisco, California 94104

Mail orders for all other parts of the world to:
Jossey-Bass Limited
28 Banner Street
London EC1Y 8QE

New Directions for Methodology of Social and Behavioral Science Series
Donald W. Fiske, *Editor-in-Chief*

MSBS1   *Unobtrusive Measurement Today,* Lee Sechrest
MSBS2   *Methods for Studying Person-Situation Interactions,* Lynn R. Kahle
MSBS3   *Realizations of Brunswik's Representative Design,* Kenneth R. Hammond, Nancy E. Wascoe
MSBS4   *Fallible Judgment in Behavioral Research,* Richard A. Shweder
MSBS5   *Quantitative Assessment of Research Domains,* Robert Rosenthal
MSBS6   *Issues in Aggregation,* Karlene H. Roberts, Leigh Burstein
MSBS7   *Biopolitics: Ethological and Physiological Approaches,* Meredith W. Watts
MSBS8   *Generalizing from Laboratory to Life,* Irwin Silverman
MSBS9   *Problems with Language Imprecision,* Donald W. Fiske
MSBS10 *Ethics of Human Subject Research,* Allan J. Kimmel

WITHDRAWN

LIBRARY
College of St. Scholastica
Duluth, Minnesota 55811

Contents

Editor's Notes   1
Robin M. Hogarth

Chapter 1. The Framing of Decisions and the Psychology of Choice   3
Amos Tversky, Daniel Kahneman
Choices are affected by the way in which decisions are framed.

Chapter 2. Response Mode, Framing, and Information-Processing   21
Effects in Risk Assessment
Paul Slovic, Baruch Fischhoff, Sarah Lichtenstein
The frame one adopts affects attitudes toward risk.

Chapter 3. The Problem of the Problem   37
J. W. Getzels
Without questions, what would the answers be?

Chapter 4. Interrogating Eyewitnesses — Good Questions and Bad   51
Elizabeth F. Loftus
Questions help and hinder eyewitness accuracy.

Chapter 5. Question-Wording Effects in Surveys   65
Norman M. Bradburn
How does question-wording affect surveys?

Chapter 6. The Importance of Context in Understanding Discourse   77
Tom Trabasso
Understanding discourse depends upon understanding context.

Chapter 7. On the Surprise and Delight of Inconsistent Responses   91
Robin M. Hogarth
Do not overlook the importance of inconsistency.

Index   105

LIBRARY
College of St. Scholastica
Duluth, Minnesota 55811

Editor's Notes

It is well known that people often respond inconsistently to the same question asked at different times and that different forms of semantically identical questions can induce systematically different responses. Less well known, however, are the conditions under which inconsistencies and distortions occur. This sourcebook examines and reviews progress that has been made in several substantive areas where question framing is of paramount importance. Attesting to the adage that question begets response, the several chapters offer theoretical suggestions and empirical evidence that illuminate this process.

The first two chapters examine how the formulation of a problem affects processes of judgment and choice. Amos Tversky and Daniel Kahneman illustrate that psychological principles underlying the perception of decisions, together with the evaluation of probabilities and outcomes, produce systematic shifts—including reversals—in preference when the same choice is posed in different ways. May the wording of our usual questions similarly affect the answers of our respondents? Paul Slovic, Baruch Fischoff, and Sarah Lichtenstein elaborate on these processes and provide further illustrations in relation to the assessment of risk. Both chapters reinforce the point that normative guides to decision making are well developed for problems that have been formulated but that no theory exists to aid people in finding the appropriate frame. Since framing effects are important, adoption of a decision frame, for oneself or for others, becomes an ethically significant act.

The importance of the question that one asks oneself in decision making and problem solving is further stressed by J. W. Getzels. This chapter is illustrated with examples from the fields of scientific discovery, artistic achievement, and administrative practice. As Getzels points out, after witnessing the successful resolution of dilemmas, we tend to admire the solutions. Frequently, however, the questions that led to the solutions are more worthy of our respect.

Eyewitness interrogation and surveys, two areas that depend heavily on the collection of facts and opinions from others, are discussed in chapters by Elizabeth F. Loftus and Norman M. Bradburn, respectively. Loftus reviews past and current work on questioning effects and illustrates that memory of past events can be systematically distorted by questions asked after the event. In particular, questions containing logical presuppositions can induce responses that bear no relation to fact. Bradburn makes the point that in large surveys, responses are often robust over changes in the form of the question used; however, subtle and sometimes important changes in meaning can be induced by way of internal question wording, differential use of response categories, and context.

Tom Trabasso illustrates the fact that people do not act like computers in decoding unique messages from specific stimuli. Rather, they depend heavily both on prior knowledge and on contextual cues in attributing meaning to both speech and text. In the absence of contextual cues, people can fail to comprehend a given passage and subsequently will be unable to recall specific details.

Finally, Robin M. Hogarth emphasizes that although inconsistencies in response can lead to inferential errors, inconsistency does have functional significance in environments where one is uncertain of the meaning of particular stimuli. Hogarth discusses the use that people make of causal reasoning in attributing meaning to stimuli and comments on the advantages and disadvantages of the mind's need to establish order out of chaos.

Robin M. Hogarth
Editor

Robin M. Hogarth is associate professor of behavioral science in the Graduate School of Business, University of Chicago, where he works in the Center for Decision Research.

Systematic reversals of preference are observed
when a decision problem is framed in different ways.

The Framing of Decisions and the Psychology of Choice

Amos Tversky
Daniel Kahneman

Explanations and predictions of people's choices, in everyday life as well as in the social sciences, are often founded on the assumption of human rationality. The definition of rationality has been much debated, but there is general agreement that rational choices should satisfy some elementary requirements of consistency and coherence. In this chapter, we describe decision problems in which people systematically violate the requirements of consistency and coherence, and we trace these violations to the psychological principles that govern the perception of decision problems and the evaluation of options.

A decision problem is defined by the acts or options among which one must choose, the possible outcomes or consequences of these acts, and the contingencies of conditional probabilities that relate outcomes to acts. We use the term *decision frame* to refer to the decision maker's conception of the acts, outcomes, and contingencies associated with a particular choice. The frame that a decision maker adopts is controlled partly by the formulation of the problem

This work was supported by the Office of Naval Research under contract N00014-79-C-0077 to Stanford University. This material is reprinted with permission from *Science,* 1981, *211,* 453–458. Copyright 1981 by the American Association for the Advancement of Science.

R. Hogarth (Ed.). *New Directions for Methodology of Social and Behavioral Science: Question Framing and Response Consistency,* no. 11. San Francisco: Jossey-Bass, March 1982.

and partly by the norms, habits, and personal characteristics of the decision maker.

It is often possible to frame a given decision problem in more than one way. Alternative frames for a decision problem may be compared to alternative perspectives on a visual scene. Veridical perception requires that the perceived relative height of two neighboring mountains, say, should not reverse with changes of the vantage point. Similarly, rational choice requires that the preference between options should not reverse with changes of frame. Because of imperfections of human perception and decision, however, changes of perspective often reverse the relative apparent size of objects and the relative desirability of options.

We have obtained systematic reversals of preference by variations in the framing of acts, contingencies, or outcomes. These effects have been observed in a variety of problems and in the choices of different groups of respondents. Here we present selected illustrations of preference reversals, with data obtained from students at Stanford University and at the University of British Columbia who answered brief questionnaires in a classroom setting. The total number of respondents for each problem is denoted by N, and the percentage who chose each option is indicated in brackets.

The effect of variations in framing is illustrated in problems 1 and 2.

Problem 1 [N = 152]. Imagine that the U.S. is preparing for the outbreak of an unusual Asian disease, which is expected to kill 600 people. Two alternative programs to combat the disease have been proposed. Assume that the exact scientific estimate of the consequences of the programs are as follows:

If program A is adopted, 200 people will be saved. [72 percent]

If program B is adopted, there is a one-third probability that 600 people will be saved, and two-thirds probability that no people will be saved. [28 percent]

Which of the two programs would you favor?

The majority choice in this problem is risk-averse: The prospect of certainly saving 200 lives is more attractive than a risky prospect of equal expected value, that is, a one-in-three chance of saving 600 lives.

A second group of respondents was given the cover story of problem 1 with a different formulation of the alternative programs, as follows:

Problem 2 [N = 155]. If program C is adopted, 400 people will die. [22 percent]

If program D is adopted, there is a one-third probability that nobody will die, and two-thirds probability that 600 people will die. [78 percent]

Which of the two programs would you favor?

The majority choice in problem 2 is risk taking: The certain death of 400 people is less acceptable than the two-in-three chance that 600 will die. The preferences in problems 1 and 2 illustrate a common pattern: Choices involving gains are often risk-averse, and choices involving losses are often risk taking. However, it is easy to see that the two problems are effectively identical. The only difference between them is that the outcomes are described in problem 1 by the number of lives saved and in problem 2 by the number of lives lost. The change is accompanied by a pronounced shift from risk aversion to risk taking. We have observed this reversal in several groups of respondents, including university faculty and physicians. Inconsistent responses to problems 1 and 2 arise from the conjunction of a framing effect with contradictory attitudes toward risks involving gains and losses. We turn now to an analysis of these attitudes.

The Evaluation of Prospects

The major theory of decision making under risk is the expected-utility model. This model is based on a set of axioms — for example, transitivity of preferences — that provide criteria for the rationality of choice. The choices of an individual who conforms to the axioms can be described in terms of the utilities of various outcomes for that individual. The utility of a risky prospect is equal to the expected utility of its outcomes, obtained by weighting the utility of each possible outcome by its probability. When faced with a choice, a rational decision maker will prefer the prospect that offers the highest expected utility (Fishburn, 1970; Raiffa, 1968; Savage, 1954; von Neumann and Morgenstern, 1947).

As will be illustrated below, people exhibit patterns of preference which appear incompatible with expected-utility theory. We have presented elsewhere (Kahneman and Tversky, 1979) a descriptive model, called *prospect theory,* which modifies expected-utility theory so as to accommodate these observations. We distinguish two phases in the choice process: an initial phase in which acts, outcomes, and contingencies are framed, and a subsequent phase of evaluation. (The framing phase includes various editing operations that are applied to simplify prospects; for example, by combining events or outcomes or by discarding negligible components.) For simplicity, we restrict the formal treatment of the theory to choices involving stated numerical probabilities and quantitative outcomes, such as money, time, or number of lives.

Consider a prospect that yields outcome x with probability p, outcome y

with probability q, and the status quo with probability $1 - p - q$. According to prospect theory, there are values $v(.)$ associated with outcomes, and decision weights $\pi(.)$ associated with probabilities, such that the overall value of the prospect equals $\pi(p)\, v(x) + \pi(q)\, v(y)$. A slightly different equation should be applied if all outcomes of a prospect are on the same side of the zero point. (Specifically, if $p + q = 1$ and either $x > y > 0$ or $x < y < 0$, the equation is replaced by $v(y) + \pi(p)[v(x) - v(y)]$, so that decision weights are not applied to sure outcomes.)

In prospect theory, outcomes are expressed as positive or negative deviations (gains or losses) from a neutral reference outcome, which is assigned a value of zero. Although subjective values differ among individuals and attributes, we propose that the value function is commonly S-shaped, concave above the reference point and convex below it, as illustrated in Figure 1. For example, the difference in subjective value between gains of $10 and $20 is greater than the subjective difference between gains of $110 and $120. The same relation between value differences holds for the corresponding losses. Another property of the value function is that the response to losses is more extreme than the response to gains. The displeasure associated with losing a sum of money is generally greater than the pleasure associated with winning the same amount, as is reflected in people's reluctance to accept fair bets on a toss of a coin. Several studies of decision (Eraker and Sox, in press; Fishburn and Kochenberger, 1979; Kahneman and Tversky, 1979; Laughhunn, Payne, and Crum, 1980; Payne, Laughhunn, and Crum, 1980) and judgment (Galanter and Pliner, 1974) have confirmed these properties of the value function. The extension of the proposed value function to multiattribute options,

Figure 1. A Hypothetical Value Function

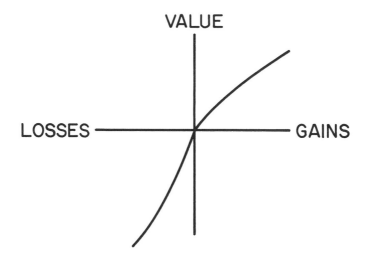

with or without risk, deserves careful analysis. In particular, indifference curves between dimensions of loss may be concave upward, even when the value functions for the separate losses are both convex, because of marked subadditivity between dimensions.

The second major departure of prospect theory from the expected-utility model involves the treatment of probabilities. In expected-utility theory, the utility of an uncertain outcome is weighted by its probability; in prospect theory, the value of an uncertain outcome is multiplied by a decision weight $\pi(p)$, which is a monotonic function of p but is not a probability. The weighting function π has the following properties. First, impossible events are discarded, that is, $\pi(0) = 0$, and the scale is normalized so that $\pi(1) = 1$, but the function is not well behaved near the endpoints. Second, for low probabilities $\pi(p) > p$, but $\pi(p) + \pi(1-p) \leq 1$. Thus, low probabilities are overweighted, moderate and high probabilities are underweighted, and the latter effect is more pronounced than the former. Third, $\pi(pq)/\pi(p) < \pi(pqr)/\pi(pr)$ for all $0 < p, q, r \leq 1$. That is, for any fixed probability ratio q, the ratio of decision weights is closer to unity when the probabilities are low than when they are high, for example, $\pi(.1)/\pi(.2) > \pi(.4)/\pi(.8)$. A hypothetical weighting function that satisfies these properties is shown in Figure 2. The major qualitative properties of decision weights can be extended to cases in which the probabilities of outcomes are subjectively assessed rather than explicitly given. In these situations, however, decision weights may also be affected by other characteristics of an event, such as ambiguity or vagueness (Ellsberg, 1961; Fellner, 1965).

Figure 2. A Hypothetical Weighting Function

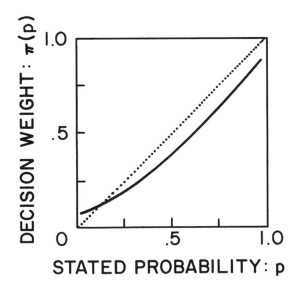

STATED PROBABILITY: p

Prospect theory, and the scales illustrated in Figures 1 and 2, should be viewed as an approximate, incomplete, and simplified description of the evaluation of risky prospects. Although the properties of v and π summarize a common pattern of choice, they are not universal; the preferences of some individuals are not well described by an S-shaped value function and a consistent set of decision weights. The simultaneous measurement of values and decision weights involves serious experimental and statistical difficulties. The scaling of v and π by pair comparisons requires a large number of observations. The procedure of pricing gambles is more convenient for scaling purposes, but it is subject to a severe anchoring bias: The ordering of gambles by their cash equivalents diverges systematically from the preference order observed in direct comparisons (Lichtenstein and Slovic, 1971).

If π and v were linear throughout, the preference order between options would be independent of the framing of acts, outcomes, or contingencies. Because of the characteristic nonlinearities of π and v, however, different frames can lead to different choices. The next three sections describe reversals of preference caused by variations in the framing of acts, contingencies, and outcomes.

The Framing of Acts

Problem 3 (N = 150]. Imagine that you face the following pair of concurrent decisions. First examine both decisions, then indicate the options you prefer.

Decision i. Choose between (A) a sure gain of $240 [84 percent] and (B) a 25 percent chance to gain $1,000, with a 75 percent chance to gain nothing [16 percent]

Decision ii. Choose between (C) a sure loss of $750 [13 percent] and (D) a 75 percent chance to lose $1,000, with a 25 percent chance to lose nothing [87 percent]

The majority choice in decision i is risk-averse: A riskless prospect is preferred to a risky prospect of equal or greater expected value. In contrast, the majority choice in decision ii is risk taking: A risky prospect is preferred to a riskless prospect of equal expected value. This pattern of risk aversion in choices involving gains and risk seeking in choices involving losses is attributable to the properties of v and π. Because the value function is S-shaped, the value associated with a gain of $240 is greater than 24 percent of the value associated with a gain of $1,000, and the (negative) value associated with a loss of $750 is smaller than 75 percent of the value associated with a loss of $1,000. Thus, the shape of the value function contributes to risk aversion in decision i and to risk seeking in decision ii. Moreover, the underweighting of moderate and high probabilities contributes to the relative attractiveness of the sure gain in decision i and to the relative aversiveness of the sure loss in decision ii. The same analysis applies to problems 1 and 2.

Because decisions i and ii were presented together, the respondents had in effect to choose one prospect from the set: A and C, B and C, A and D, B and D. The most common pattern (A and D) was chosen by 73 percent of respondents, while the least popular pattern (B and C) was chosen by only 3 percent of respondents. However, the combination of B and C is definitely superior to the combination A and D, as is readily seen in problem 4.

> *Problem 4* [N = 86]. Choose between: (A and D) a 25 percent chance to win $240 and a 75 percent chance to lose $760 [0 percent] and (B and C) a 25 percent chance to win $250 and a 75 percent chance to lose $750 [100 percent]

When the prospects were combined and the dominance of the second option became obvious, all respondents chose the superior option. The popularity of the inferior option in problem 3 implies that this problem was framed as a pair of separate choices. The respondents apparently failed to entertain the possibility that the conjunction of two seemingly reasonable choices could lead to an untenable result.

The violations of dominance observed in problem 3 do not disappear in the presence of monetary incentives. A different group of respondents who answered a modified version of problem 3, with real payoffs, produced a similar pattern of choices. A new group of respondents (N = 126) was presented with a modified version of problem 3, in which the outcomes were reduced by a factor of fifty. The participants were informed that the gambles would actually be played by tossing a pair of fair coins and that one participant in ten would be selected at random to play the gambles of his or her choice. To ensure a positive return for the entire set, a third decision, yielding only positive outcomes, was added. These payoff conditions did not alter the pattern of preferences observed in the hypothetical problem: 67 percent of respondents chose prospect A, and 86 percent chose prospect D. The dominated combination of A and D was chosen by 60 percent of respondents, and only 6 percent favored the dominant combination of B and C. Other authors have also reported that violations of the rules of rational choice, originally observed in hypothetical questions, were not eliminated by payoffs (Grether, 1980; Grether and Plott, 1979; Lichtenstein and Slovic, 1973; Lieblich and Lieblich, 1969).

We suspect that many concurrent decisions in the real world are framed independently, and that the preference order would often be reversed if the decisions were combined. The respondents in problem 3 failed to combine options, although the integration was relatively simple and was encouraged by instructions. (For other demonstrations of a reluctance to integrate concurrent options, see Payne and Braunstein, 1971; Slovic and Lichtenstein, 1968). The complexity of practical problems of concurrent decisions, such as portfolio selection, would prevent people from integrating options without computational aids, even if they were inclined to do so.

The Framing of Contingencies

The next trio of problems illustrates the framing of contingencies. Each problem was presented to a different group of respondents. Each group was told that one participant in ten, preselected at random, would actually be playing for money. Chance events were realized in the respondents' presence, by drawing a single ball from a bag containing a known proportion of balls of the winning color, and the winners were paid immediately.

Problem 5 [N = 77]. Which of the following options do you prefer: (A) a sure win of $30 (78 percent) or (B) an 80 percent chance to win $45? [22 percent]

Problem 6 [N = 85]. Consider the following two-stage game. In the first stage, there is a 75 percent chance to end the game without winning anything, and a 25 percent chance to move into the second stage. If you reach the second stage, you have a choice between (C) a sure win of $30 [74 percent] and (D) an 80 percent chance to win $45 (26 percent]

Your choice must be made before the game starts; that is, before the outcome of the first stage is known. Please indicate the option you prefer.

Problem 7 [N = 81]. Which of the following options do you prefer: (E) a 25 percent chance to win $30 [42 percent] or (F) a 20 percent chance to win $45? [58 percent]

Let us examine the structure of these problems. First, note that problems 6 and 7 are identical in terms of probabilities and outcomes, because prospect C offers a .25 chance to win $30 and prospect D offers a probability of .25 × .80 = .20 to win $45. Consistency therefore requires that the same choice be made in problems 6 and 7. Second, note that problem 6 differs from problem 5 only by the introduction of a preliminary stage. If the second stage of the game is reached, then problem 6 reduces to problem 5; if the game ends at the first stage, the decision does not affect the outcome. Hence, there seems to be no reason to make a different choice in problems 5 and 6. By this logical analysis, problem 6 is equivalent to problem 7 on the one hand and problem 5 on the other. The participants, however, responded similarly to problems 5 and 6 but differently to problem 7. This pattern of responses exhibits two phenomena of choice: the certainty effect and the pseudocertainty effect.

The contrast between problems 5 and 7 illustrates a phenomenon discovered by Allais (1953), which we have labeled *the certainty effect:* A reduction of the probability of an outcome by a constant factor has more impact when the outcome was initially certain than when it was merely probable (Allais,

1953; MacCrimmon and Larsson, 1979). Prospect theory attributes this effect to the properties of π. It is easy to verify by applying the equation of prospect theory to problems 5 and 7, that people for whom the value ratio $v(30)/v(45)$ lies between the weight ratios $\pi(.20)/\pi(.25)$, and $\pi(.80)/\pi(1.0)$ will prefer A to B and F to E, contrary to expected-utility theory. Prospect theory does not predict a reversal of preference for every individual in problems 5 and 7. It only requires that an individual who has no preference between A and B prefer F to E. For group data, the theory predicts the observed directional shift of preference between the two problems.

The first stage of problem 6 yields the same outcome (no gain) for both acts. Consequently, we propose, people evaluate the options conditionally, as if the second stage had been reached. In this framing, of course, problem 6 reduces to problem 5. More generally, we suggest that a decision problem is evaluated conditionally when there is a state in which all acts yield the same outcome, such as failing to reach the second stage of the game in problem 6, and the stated probabilities of other outcomes are conditional on the nonoccurrence of this state.

The striking discrepancy between the responses to problems 6 and 7, which are identical in outcomes and probabilities, could be described as a pseudocertainty effect. The prospect yielding $30 is relatively more attractive in problem 6 than in problem 7, as if it had the advantage of certainty. The sense of certainty associated with option C is illusory, however, since the gain is in fact contingent on reaching the second stage of the game.

Another group of respondents (N = 205) was presented with all three problems, in different orders, without monetary payoffs. The joint frequency distribution of choices in problems 5, 6, and 7 was as follows: ACE, 22; ACF, 65; ADE, 4; ADF, 20; BCE, 7; BCF, 18; BDE, 17; BDF, 52. These data confirm in a within-subject design the analysis of conditional evaluation proposed in the text. More than 75 percent of respondents made compatible choices (AC or BD) in problems 5 and 6, and less than half made compatible choices in problems 6 and 7 (CE or DF) or 5 and 7 (AE or BF). The elimination of payoffs in these questions reduced risk aversion but did not substantially alter the effects of certainty and pseudocertainty.

We have observed the certainty effect in several sets of problems, with outcomes ranging from vacation trips to the loss of human lives. In the negative domain, certainty exaggerates the aversiveness of losses that are certain relative to losses that are merely probable. In a question dealing with the response to an epidemic, for example, most respondents found a sure loss of 75 lives more aversive than an 80 percent chance to lose 100 lives but preferred a 10 percent chance to lose 75 lives to an 8 percent chance to lose 100 lives, contrary to expected-utility theory.

We also obtained the pseudocertainty effect in several studies where the description of the decision problems favored conditional evaluation. Pseudocertainty can be induced either by a sequential formulation, as in problem 6, or by the introduction of causal contingencies. In another version of the epidemic problem, for instance, respondents were told that risk to life existed only in the event (probability .10) that the disease was carried by a particular virus. Two alternative programs were said to yield a sure loss of 75 lives or an 80 percent chance to lose 100 lives if the critical virus was involved, and no loss of life in the event (probability .90) that the disease was carried by another virus. In effect, the respondents were asked to choose between a 10 percent chance of losing 75 lives and an 8 percent chance of losing 100 lives, but their preferences were the same as when the choice was between a sure loss of 75 lives and an 80 percent chance of losing 100 lives. A conditional framing was evidently adopted, in which the contingency of the noncritical virus was eliminated, giving rise to a pseudocertainty effect. The certainty effect reveals attitudes toward risk that are inconsistent with the axioms of rational choice, whereas the pseudocertainty effect violates the more fundamental requirement that preferences should be independent of problem description.

Many significant decisions concern actions that reduce or eliminate the probability of a hazard, at some cost. The shape of π in the range of low probabilities suggests that a protective action which reduces the probability of a harm from 1 percent to zero, say, will be valued more highly than an action that reduces the probability of the same harm from 2 percent to 1 percent. Indeed, probabilistic insurance, which reduces the probability of loss by half, is judged to be worth less than half the price of regular insurance that eliminates the risk altogether (Kahneman and Tversky, 1979).

It is often possible to frame protective action in either conditional or unconditional form. For example, an insurance policy that covers fire but not flood could be evaluated either as full protection against the specific risk of fire or as a reduction in the overall probability of property loss. The preceding analysis suggests that insurance should appear more attractive when it is presented as the elimination of risk than when it is described as a reduction of risk. As Slovic, Fischhoff, and Lichtenstein report in this sourcebook, a hypothetical vaccine that reduces the probability of contracting a disease from .20 to .10 is less attractive if it is described as effective in half the cases than if it is presented as fully effective against one of two (exclusive and equiprobable) virus strains that produce identical symptoms. In accord with the present analysis of pseudocertainty, the respondents valued full protection against an identified virus more than probabilistic protection against the disease.

The preceding discussion highlights the sharp contrast between lay responses to the reduction and the elimination of risk. Because no form of protective action can cover all risks to human welfare, all insurance is essentially probabilistic: It reduces but does not eliminate risk. The probabilistic nature of insurance is commonly masked by formulations that emphasize the completeness of protection against identified harms, but the sense of security that such formulations provide is an illusion of conditional framing. It appears that insurance is bought as protection against worry, not only against risk, and that worry can be manipulated by the labeling of outcomes and by the framing of contingencies. It is not easy to determine whether people value the elimination of risk too much or the reduction of risk too little. The contrasting attitudes to the two forms of protective action, however, are difficult to justify on normative grounds. (For further discussion of rationality in protective action, see Kunreuther and others, 1978.)

The Framing of Outcomes

Outcomes are commonly perceived as positive or negative in relation to a reference outcome that is judged neutral. Variations of the reference point can therefore determine whether a given outcome is evaluated as a gain or as a loss. Because the value function is generally concave for gains, convex for losses, and steeper for losses than for gains, shifts of reference can change the value difference between outcomes and thereby reverse the preference order between options (Eraker and Sox, in press; Fishburn and Kochenberger, 1979; Laughhunn, Payne, and Crum, 1980; Payne, Laughhunn, and Crum, 1980). Problems 1 and 2 illustrate a preference reversal induced by a shift of reference that transformed gains into losses.

For another example, consider a person who has spent an afternoon at the racetrack, has already lost $140, and is considering a $10 bet on a 15:1 long shot in the last race. This decision can be framed in two ways, which correspond to two natural reference points. If the status quo is the reference point, the outcomes of the bet are framed as a gain of $140 and a loss of $10. However, it may be more natural to view the present state as a loss of $140 for the betting day, and accordingly frame the last bet as a chance to return to the reference point or to increase the loss to $150. Prospect theory implies that the latter frame will produce more risk seeking than the former. Hence, people who do not adjust their reference point as they lose are expected to take bets that they would normally find unacceptable. This analysis is supported by the observation that bets on long shots are most popular on the last race of the day (McGlothlin, 1956).

Because the value function is steeper for losses than for gains, a difference between options will loom larger when it is framed as a disadvantage of one option rather than as an advantage of the other option. An interesting example of such an effect in a riskless context has been noted by Thaler (1980). In a debate on a proposal to pass to the consumer some of the costs associated with the processing of credit card purchases, representatives of the credit card industry requested that the price difference be labeled a cash discount rather than a credit card surcharge. The two labels induce different reference points by implicitly designating as normal reference the higher or the lower of the two prices. Because losses loom larger than gains, consumers are less willing to accept a surcharge than to forego a discount. A similar effect has been observed in experimental studies of insurance: The proportion of respondents who preferred a sure loss to a larger probable loss was significantly greater when the former was called an insurance premium (Fischhoff, Slovic, and Lichtenstein, 1980; Hershey and Schoemaker, 1980).

These observations highlight the lability of reference outcomes, as well as their role in decision making. In the examples discussed so far, the neutral reference point was identified by the labeling of outcomes. A diversity of factors determines the reference outcome in everyday life. The reference outcome is usually a state to which one has adapted; it is sometimes set by social norms and expectations; it sometimes corresponds to a level of aspiration, which may or may not be realistic.

We have dealt so far with elementary outcomes, such as gains or losses in a single attribute. In many situations, however, an action gives rise to a compound outcome, which joins a series of changes in a single attribute, such as a sequence of monetary gains and losses, or a set of concurrent changes in several attributes. To describe the framing and evaluation of compound outcomes, we use the notion of a psychological account, defined as an outcome frame which specifies both the set of elementary outcomes that are evaluated jointly and the manner in which they are combined, and a reference outcome that is considered neutral or normal. In the account that is set up for the purchase of a car, for example, the cost of the purchase is not treated as a loss, nor is the car viewed as a gift. Rather, the transaction as a whole is evaluated as positive, negative, or neutral, depending on such factors as the performance of the car and the price of similar cars in the market. A closely related treatment has been offered by Thaler (1980).

We propose that people generally evaluate acts in terms of a minimal account, which includes only the direct consequences of the act. The minimal account associated with the decision to accept a gamble, for example, includes the money won or lost in that gamble and excludes other assets or the outcome of previous gambles. People commonly adopt minimal accounts because this mode of framing simplifies evaluation and reduces cognitive strain, reflects the intuition that consequences should be causally linked to acts, and matches the properties of hedonic experience, which is more sensitive to desirable and undesirable changes than to steady states.

There are situations, however, in which the outcomes of an act affect the balance in an account that was previously set up by a related act. In these cases, the decision at hand may be evaluated in terms of a more inclusive account, as in the case of the bettor who views the last race in the context of earlier losses. More generally, a sunk-cost effect arises when a decision is referred to an existing account in which the current balance is negative. Because of the nonlinearities of the evaluation process, the minimal account and a more inclusive one often lead to different choices.

Problems 8 and 9 illustrate another class of situations in which an existing account affects a decision:

Problem 8 [N = 183]. Imagine that you have decided to see a play where admission is $10 per ticket. As you enter the theater, you discover that you have lost a $10 bill.

Would you still pay $10 for a ticket for the play?
Yes [88 percent]   No [12 percent]

Problem 9 [N = 200]. Imagine that you have decided to see a play and paid the admission price of $10 per ticket. As you enter the theater, you discover that you have lost the ticket. The seat was not marked, and the ticket cannot be recovered.

Would you pay $10 for another ticket?
Yes [46 percent]   No [54 percent]

The marked difference between the responses to problems 8 and 9 is an effect of psychological accounting. We propose that the purchase of a new ticket in problem 9 is entered in the account that was set up by the purchase of the original ticket. In terms of this account, the expense required to see the show is $20, a cost which many of our respondents apparently found excessive. In problem 8, however, the loss of $10 is not linked specifically to the ticket purchase, and its effect on the decision is accordingly slight.

The following problem, based on examples by Savage (1954, p. 103) and Thaler (1980), further illustrates the effect of embedding an option in different accounts. Two versions of this problem were presented to different groups of subjects. One group (N = 93) was given the values that appear in parentheses, and the other group (N = 88) was given the values shown in brackets.

Problem 10. Imagine that you are about to purchase a jacket for ($125) [$15], and a calculator for ($15) [$125]. The calculator salesman informs you that the calculator you wish to buy is on sale for ($10) [$120] at the other branch of the store, located twenty minutes' drive away. Would you make the trip to the other store?

The responses to the two versions of problem 10 were markedly different: 68 percent of the respondents were willing to make an extra trip to save $5 on a $15 calculator; only 29 percent were willing to exert the same effort when the price of the calculator was $125. Evidently, the respondents do not frame problem 10 in the minimal account, which involves only a benefit of $5 and a cost of some inconvenience. Instead, they evaluate the potential savings in a more inclusive account, which includes the purchase of the calculator but not the purchase of the jacket. By the curvature of v, a discount of $5 has a greater impact when the price of the calculator is low than when it is high.

A closely related observation has been reported by Pratt, Wise, and Zeckhauser (1979), who found that the variability of the prices at which a given product is sold by different stores is roughly proportional to the mean price of that product. The same pattern was observed for both frequently and infrequently purchased items. Overall, a ratio of 2:1 in the mean price of two products is associated with a ratio of 1.86:1 in the standard deviation of the respective quoted prices. If the effort that consumers exert to save each dollar on a purchase, for instance by a phone call, were independent of price, the dispersion of quoted prices should be about the same for all products. In contrast, the data of Pratt, Wise, and Zeckhauser (1979) are consistent with the hypothesis that consumers hardly exert more effort to save $15 on a $150 purchase than to save $5 on a $50 dollar purchase (Thaler, 1980). Many readers will recognize the temporary devaluation of money which facilitates extra spending and reduces the significance of small discounts in the context of a large expenditure, such as buying a house or a car. This paradoxical variation in the value of money is incompatible with the standard analysis of consumer behavior.

Discussion

In this chapter, we have presented a series of demonstrations in which seemingly inconsequential changes in the formulation of choice problems caused significant shifts of preference. The inconsistencies were traced to the interaction of two sets of factors: variations in the framing of acts, contingencies, and outcomes, and the characteristic nonlinearities of values and decision weights. The demonstrated effects are large and systematic, although by no means universal. They occur when the outcomes concern the loss of human lives as well as in choices about money; they are not restricted to hypothetical questions and are not eliminated by monetary incentives.

Earlier, we compared the dependence of preferences on frames to the dependence of perceptual appearance on perspective. If while traveling in a mountain range you notice that the apparent relative height of mountain peaks varies with your vantage point, you will conclude that some impressions of relative height must be erroneous, even when you have no access to the correct answer. Similarly, one may discover that the relative attractiveness of options varies when the same decision problem is framed in different ways. Such a discovery will normally lead the decision maker to reconsider the original preferences, even when there is no simple way to resolve the inconsistency. The susceptibility to perspective effects is of special concern in the domain of decision making because of the absence of objective standards, such as the true height of mountains.

The metaphor of changing perspective can be applied to other phenomena of choice, in addition to the framing effects with which we have been concerned here (Fischhoff, Slovic, and Lichtenstein, 1980). The problem of self-control is naturally construed in these terms. The story of Ulysses' request to be bound to the mast of the ship in anticipation of the irresistible temptation of the Sirens' call is often used as a paradigm case (Ainslie, 1975; Elster, 1979; Strotz, 1955–1956; Thaler and Shifrin, 1981). In this example of precommitment, an action taken in the present renders inoperative an anticipated future preference. An unusual feature of the problem of intertemporal conflict is that the agent who views a problem from a particular temporal perspective is also aware of the conflicting views that future perspectives will offer. In most other situations, decision makers are not normally aware of the potential effects of different decision frames on their preferences.

The perspective metaphor highlights four aspects of the psychology of choice. Individuals who face a decision problem and have a definite preference, first, might have a different preference in a different framing of the same problem; second, are normally unaware of alternative frames and of their potential effects on the relative attractiveness of options; third, would wish their preferences to be independent of frame; but, fourth, are often uncertain how to resolve detected inconsistencies (Slovic and Tversky, 1974). In some cases (such as problems 3 and 4 and perhaps problems 8 and 9) the advantage of one frame becomes evident once the competing frames are compared, but in other cases (problems 1 and 2 and problems 6 and 7) it is not obvious which preferences should be abandoned.

These observations do not imply that preference reversals or other errors of choice or judgment are necessarily irrational (Einhorn and Hogarth, 1981; Nisbett and Ross, 1980; Slovic, Fischhoff, and Lichtenstein, 1977; Tversky and Kahneman, 1974). Like other intellectual limitations, discussed by Simon (1955, 1956) under the heading of "bounded rationality," the practice of acting on the most readily available frame can sometimes be justified by reference to the mental effort required to explore alternative frames and avoid potential inconsistencies. However, we propose that the details of the phenomena described in this chapter are better explained by prospect theory and by an analysis of framing than by ad hoc appeals to the notion of cost of thinking.

The work described here has been concerned primarily with the descriptive question of how decisions are made, but the psychology of choice is also relevant to the normative question of how decisions ought to be made. In order to avoid the difficult problem of justifying values, the modern theory of rational choice has adopted the coherence of specific preferences as the sole criterion of rationality. This approach enjoins the decision maker to resolve inconsistencies but offers no guidance on how to do so. It implicitly assumes that the decision maker who carefully answers the question "What do I really want?" will eventually achieve coherent preferences. However, the susceptibility of preferences to variations of framing raises doubt about the feasibility and adequacy of the coherence criterion.

Consistency is only one aspect of the lay notion of rational behavior. As noted by March (1978), the common conception of rationality also requires that preferences or utilities for particular outcomes should be predictive of the experiences of satisfaction or displeasure associated with their occurrence. Thus, a man could be judged irrational either because his preferences are contradictory or because his desires and aversions do not reflect his pleasures and pains. The predictive criterion of rationality can be applied to resolve inconsistent preferences and to improve the quality of decisions. A predictive orientation encourages the decision maker to focus on future experience and to ask "What will I feel then?" rather than "What do I want now?" The former question, when answered with care, can be the more useful guide in difficult decisions. In particular, predictive considerations may be applied to select the decision frame that best represents the hedonic experience of outcomes.

Further complexities arise in the normative analysis because the framing of an action sometimes affects the actual experience of its outcomes. For example, framing outcomes in terms of overall wealth or welfare rather than in terms of specific gains and losses may attenuate one's emotional response to an occasional loss. Similarly, the experience of a change for the worse may vary if the change is framed as an uncompensated loss or as a cost incurred to achieve some benefit. The framing of acts and outcomes can also reflect the acceptance or rejection of responsibility for particular consequences, and the deliberate manipulation of framing is commonly used as an instrument of self-control (Ainslie, 1975; Elster, 1979; Strotz, 1955–1956; Thaler and Shifrin, 1981). When framing influences the experience of consequences, the adoption of a decision frame is an ethically significant act.

References

Ainslie, G. "Specious Reward: A Behavioral Theory of Impulsiveness and Impulse Control." *Psychological Bulletin,* 1975, *82,* 463–496.

Allais, M. "Le comportement de l'homme devant le risque: Critique des postulats et axiomes de l'école américaine." *Econometrica,* 1953, *21,* 503–546.

Einhorn, H. J., and Hogarth, R. M. "Behavioral Decision Theory: Processes of Judgment and Choice." *Annual Review of Psychology,* 1981, *32,* 53–88.

Ellsberg, D. "Risk, Ambiguity, and the Savage Axioms." *Quarterly Journal of Economics,* 1961, *75,* 643–669.

Elster, J. *Ulysses and the Sirens: Studies in Rationality and Irrationality.* London: Cambridge University Press, 1979.

Eraker, S. A., and Sox, H. C. "Assessment of Patients' Preferences for Therapeutic Outcomes." *Medical Decision Making,* in press.

Fellner, W. *Probability and Profit: A Study of Economic Behavior Along Bayesian Lines.* Homewood, Ill.: Irwin, 1965.

Fishburn, P. C. *Utility Theory for Decision Making.* New York: Wiley, 1970.

Fishburn, P. C., and Kochenberger, G. A. "Two-Piece von Neumann-Morgenstern Utility Functions." *Decision Sciences,* 1979, *10,* 503–518.

Fischhoff, B., Slovic, P., and Lichtenstein, S. "Knowing What You Want: Measuring Labile Values." In T. Wallsten (Ed.), *Cognitive Processes in Choice and Decision Behavior.* Hillsdale, N.J.: Erlbaum, 1980.

Galanter, E., and Pliner, P. "Cross-Modality Matching of Money Against Other Continua." In H. R. Moskowitz and others (Eds.), *Sensation and Measurement.* Dordrecht: Reidel, 1974.

Grether, D. M. "Bayes Rule as a Descriptive Model: The Representativeness Heuristic." *Quarterly Journal of Economics,* 1980, *95,* 537–557.

Grether, D. M., and Plott, C. R. "Economic Theory of Choice and the Preference Reversal Phenomenon." *American Economic Review,* 1979, *69,* 623–638.

Hershey, J. C., and Schoemaker, P. J. H. "Risk Taking and Problem Context in the Domain of Losses: An Expected-Utility Analysis." *Journal of Risk and Insurance,* 1980, *47,* 111–132.

Kahneman, D., and Tversky, A. "Prospect Theory: An Analysis of Decision Under Risk." *Econometrica,* 1979, *47,* 263–291.

Kunreuther, H., and others. *Disaster Insurance Protection: Public Policy Lessons.* New York: Wiley, 1978.

Laughhunn, D. J., Payne, J. W., and Crum, R. "Managerial Risk Preferences for Below-Target Returns." *Management Science,* 1980, *26,* 1238–1249.

Lichtenstein, S., and Slovic, P. "Reversals of Preference Between Bids and Choices in Gambling Decisions." *Journal of Experimental Psychology,* 1971, *98,* 46–55.

Lichtenstein, S., and Slovic, P. "Response-Induced Reversals of Preference in Gambling: An Extended Replication in Las Vegas." *Journal of Experimental Psychology,* 1973, *101,* 16–20.

Lieblich, I., and Lieblich, A. "Effects of Different Payoff Matrices on Arithmetical Estimation Tasks: An Attempt to Produce Rationality." *Perceptual and Motor Skills,* 1969, *29,* 467–473.

MacCrimmon, K. R., and Larsson, S. "Utility Theory: Axioms Versus Paradoxes." In M. Allais and O. Hagen (Eds.), *Expected-Utility Hypotheses and the Allais Paradox,* Vol. 21. Dordrecht: Reidel, 1979.

March, J. G. "Bounded Rationality, Ambiguity, and the Engineering of Choice." *Bell Journal of Economics,* 1978, *9,* 587–608.

McGlothlin, W. H. "Stability of Choices Among Uncertain Alternatives." *American Journal of Psychology,* 1956, *69,* 604–615.

Nisbett, R. E., and Ross, L. *Human Inference: Strategies and Shortcomings of Social Judgment.* Englewood Cliffs, N.J.: Prentice-Hall, 1980.

Payne, J. W., and Braunstein, M. L. "Preferences Among Gambles with Equal Underlying Distributions." *Journal of Experimental Psychology,* 1971, *87,* 13–18.

Payne, J. W., Laughhunn, D. J., and Crum, R. "Translation of Gambles and Aspiration-Level Effects in Risky Choice Behavior." *Management Science,* 1980, *26,* 1039–1060.

Pratt, J. W., Wise, D., and Zeckhauser, R. "Price Differences in Almost Competitive Markets." *Quarterly Journal of Economics,* 1979, *93,* 189–211.

Raiffa, H. *Decision Analysis: Introductory Lectures on Choices Under Uncertainty.* Reading, Mass.: Addison-Wesley, 1968.

Savage, L. J. *The Foundations of Statistics.* New York: Wiley, 1954.

Simon, H. A. "A Behavioral Model of Rational Choice." *Quarterly Journal of Economics,* 1955, *69,* 99–118.

Simon, H. A. "Rational Choice and the Structure of the Environment." *Psychological Review,* 1956, *63,* 129–138.

Slovic, P., Fischhoff, B., and Lichtenstein, S. "Behavioral Decision Theory." *Annual Review of Psychology,* 1977, *28,* 1–39.

Slovic, P., and Lichtenstein, S. "Importance of Variance Preferences in Gambling and Decisions." *Journal of Experimental Psychology,* 1968, *78,* 646–654.

Slovic, P., and Tversky, A. "Who Accepts Savage's Axiom?" *Behavioral Science,* 1974, *14,* 368–373.

Strotz, R. "Myopia and Inconsistency in Dynamic Utility Maximization." *Review of Economic Studies,* 1955–1956, *23,* 165–180.

Thaler, R. "Toward a Positive Theory of Consumer Choice." *Journal of Economic Behavior and Organization,* 1980, *1,* 39–60.

Thaler, R., and Shifrin, H. M. "An Economic Theory of Self-Control." *Journal of Political Economy,* 1981, *89,* 392–406.

Tversky, A., and Kahneman, D. "Judgment Under Uncertainty: Heuristics and Biases." *Science,* 1974, *185,* 1124–1131.

von Neumann, J., and Morgenstern, O. *Theory of Games and Economic Behavior.* Princeton, N.J.: Princeton University Press, 1947.

Amos Tversky is professor of psychology at Stanford University.

Daniel Kahneman is professor of psychology at the University of British Columbia.

Both task features and contextual considerations affect the framing of judgment and choice.

Response Mode, Framing, and Information-Processing Effects in Risk Assessment

Paul Slovic
Baruch Fischhoff
Sarah Lichtenstein

The chapter on framing by Tversky and Kahneman in this volume demonstrates that normatively inconsequential changes in the formulation of choice problems significantly affect preferences. These effects are noteworthy because they are sizable (sometimes complete reversals of preference), because they violate important tenets of rationality, and because they influence not only behavior but how the consequences of behavior are experienced. These perturbations are traced (in prospect theory; see Kahneman and Tversky, 1979) to the interaction between the manner in which acts, contingencies, and outcomes are framed in decision problems and general propensities for treating values and uncertainty in nonlinear ways.

The authors wish to thank Amos Tversky for comments on an earlier draft of this chapter. The writing was supported by the National Science Foundation under grant PRS79-11934 to Clark University under subcontract to Perceptronics, Inc. All opinions, findings, conclusions, and recommendations expressed in this publication are those of the authors and do not necessarily reflect the views of the National Science Foundation.

R. Hogarth (Ed.). *New Directions for Methodology of Social and Behavioral Science: Question Framing and Response Consistency,* no. 11. San Francisco: Jossey-Bass, March 1982.

The present chapter begins by providing additional demonstrations of framing effects. Next, it extends the concept of framing to effects induced by changes of response mode, and it illustrates effects due to the interaction between response mode and information-processing considerations. Two specific response modes are studied in detail: judgments of single objects and choices among two or more options. Judgments are prone to influence by anchoring-and-adjustment processes, which ease the strain of integrating diverse items of information. Choices are prone to context effects that develop as a result of justification processes, through which the deliberations preceding choice are woven into a rationalization of that action. As we shall see, these processes often cause judgments and choices to be inconsistent with one another.

Response mode, framing, and information-processing considerations apply to all decision problems. However, like Tversky and Kahneman, we shall focus primarily on risk-taking decisions ranging from choices among simple gambles to complex decisions about protective actions, such as insurance, vaccination, and the use of seat belts. The studies to be described demonstrate the extreme sensitivity of judgments and decisions to subtle changes in problem format and response mode.

Concreteness and the Framing of Acts

Decision options can often be viewed in a variety of perspectives. For example, Tversky and Kahneman show in this volume that concurrent decision problems are dealt with independently, rather than as an integrated combination. Thus, choosing both a sure gain of $240 and a gamble offering a 75 percent chance of losing $1,000 and a 25 percent chance of losing nothing is not viewed as equivalent to its conjunctions: a 25 percent chance of winning $240 and a 75 percent chance of losing $760.

By failing to integrate concurrent acts, Tversky and Kahneman's subjects responded to the explicit characteristics of each act and did not perform the simple transformations necessary to effect their merger. Similar behavior has been observed in two experiments that examined the effects of explicit representation of the variance of outcomes of simple gambles. In one experiment, specially constructed gambles manipulated variance without changing the probabilities and payoffs that were explicitly displayed to the subject (Slovic and Lichtenstein, 1968). To illustrate this, consider the upper half of Figure 1, which shows two bets: a duplex bet and a standard bet, which can be termed *parallel* because both have the same stated probabilities and the same payoffs, namely .6 chance to win $2 and .4 chance to lose $2. Imagine that the bets can be played by spinning pointers on the circular discs shown in Figure 1 such that one wins or loses the amount indicated by the final position of the pointer. To play a duplex bet, one must spin the pointer on both discs. Thus, one can win and not lose, lose and not win, both win and lose, or neither win nor lose.

Figure 1. Experimental Gambles

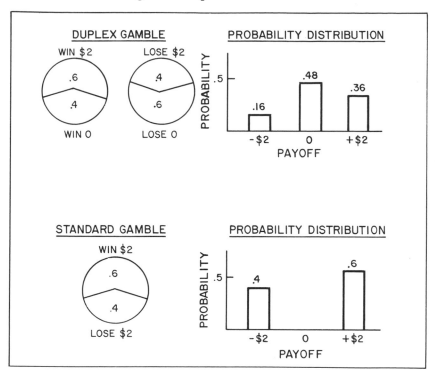

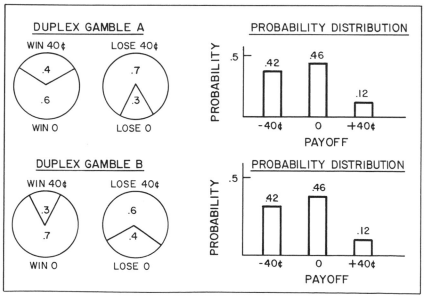

Source: Slovic and Lichtenstein (1968); Payne and Braunstein (1971).

As a consequence, the duplex bet has much less variance than its parallel standard bet. That is, the standard bet leads either to a gain or loss of $2; however, by playing the duplex bet, one has a fairly high probability of breaking even. Most subjects perceived duplex bets and their parallel standard bets as equally attractive, which suggests that their judgments were based only upon the explicitly stated probabilities and payoffs. The characteristics of the underlying distribution for the duplex bet did not exert any significant influence.

The second experiment (Payne and Braunstein, 1971) nicely complements the first. This experiment used pairs of duplex gambles with equal underlying distributions but different explicit probability values, as illustrated in the lower half of Figure 1. Subjects showed strong preferences for one member of such pairs over the other, which further demonstrates the dominance of explicit or surface information.

These two experiments illustrate a form of concrete thinking (Slovic, 1972) whereby decision makers appear to use only the information that is explicitly displayed in the formulation of the problem. Information that has to be inferred from the display or created by some mental transformation tends to be ignored. The tendency for considerations that are out of sight to be out of mind (see also Fischhoff, Slovic, and Lichtenstein, 1978) imposes a serious burden on those entrusted with presentation of risk information.

Protective Action and the Framing of Contingencies

Pseudocertainty. According to prospect theory, outcomes that are merely probable are underweighted in comparison with outcomes that are obtained with certainty. As a result, any protective action that reduces the probability of harm from, say, .01 to zero will be valued more highly than an action that reduces the probability of the same harm from .02 to .01.

In this volume, Tversky and Kahneman note that mental representations of protective actions can easily be manipulated so as to vary the apparent certainty with which they prevent harm. For example, an insurance policy that covers fire but not flood can be presented either as full protection against the specific risk of fire or as a reduction in the overall probability of property loss. Prospect theory predicts that the policy will appear more attractive in the former perspective, labeled *pseudocertainty,* in which it offers unconditional protection against a restricted set of problems.

We have tested this conjecture in the context of one particular kind of protection, vaccination. Two forms of a vaccination questionnaire were created. Form I (probabilistic protection) described a disease that was expected to afflict 20 percent of the population, and it asked people whether they would volunteer to receive a vaccine that protected half the people who received it. According to Form II (pseudocertainty), there were two mutually exclusive and equiprobable strains of the disease, each of which was expected to afflict 10 percent of the population; vaccination was said to give complete protection against one strain and no protection against the other. The 211 participants in this study were recruited by an advertisement in the University of Oregon student newspaper. Half received Form I; the other half received Form II. After reading the description, they rated the likelihood that they would get vaccinated in such a situation, using a seven-point scale ranging from 1 ("almost certainly would not get vaccinated") to 7 ("almost certainly would get vaccinated").

Although both forms indicated that vaccination reduced one's overall risk from 20 percent to 10 percent, we expected that vaccination would appear more attractive to those who received Form II (pseudocertainty) than to those who received Form I (probabilistic insurance). The results confirmed this prediction: Fifty-seven percent of those who received Form II indicated that they would get vaccinated, compared to 40 percent for those who received Form I.

The pseudocertainty effect highlights the contrast between reduction and elimination of risk. As Tversky and Kahneman have indicated, this distinction is difficult to justify on normative grounds. Moreover, manipulations of certainty would seem to have important implications for the design and description of other forms of protection, such as medical treatments, insurance, and flood- and earthquake-proofing activities.

Seat Belts. Research has demonstrated that seat belts are effective in reducing death and injury in automobile accidents and that most people are aware of this fact. However, the percentage of motorists who wear them is small, and numerous and expensive media campaigns have failed to persuade people to "buckle up for safety" (Robertson, 1976).

The reluctance of motorists to wear seat belts is puzzling to many safety officials, in light of the high personal costs of a serious accident. One clue to motorists' reluctance is the finding of Slovic and others (1977) that perceived probability of loss was a key determinant of protective action in the context of insurance decisions. Extrapolating from insurance to seat belts, Slovic, Fischhoff, and Lichtenstein (1978) argued that resistance to the wearing of seat belts was understandable in light of the extremely small probability of an accident on a single automobile trip. Because a fatal accident occurs only about once in every 3.5 million person-trips and a disabling injury only once in every 100,000 person-trips, refusing to buckle one's seat belt prior to a single trip is not unreasonable.

The risks of driving can be framed differently, however. During the course of a fifty-year lifetime of driving, the average motorist will take some 40,000 or more trips. The probability that one of these trips will end in a fatality is .01, and the probability of experiencing at least one disabling injury during this period is .33. It is as appropriate to consider these cumulative probabilities of death and disability as it is to consider the odds on a single trip. Slovic, Fischhoff, and Lichtenstein (1978) conducted a pilot study in which subjects were induced to adopt either a lifetime or a trip-by-trip perspective. Subjects in the lifetime condition responded more favorably toward use of seat belts and toward the enactment of laws requiring the wearing of seat belts or the installation of air bags. As a result of exposure to single-trip risk statistics, fewer than 10 percent of the college students surveyed claimed that their use of seat belts would be changed, but 39 percent of those exposed to the cumulative probabilities said that they expected their use of seat belts to increase. Whereas 54 percent of the persons who received single-trip information favored mandatory protection, 78 percent of those exposed to lifetime probabilities favored such a law. Whether the favorable attitudes toward seat belts engendered by a lengthened time perspective will be maintained and translated into behavior remains to be determined.

Insurance Decisions and the Framing of Outcomes

Traditionally, explanations of insurance decisions have been based upon utility theory (Friedman and Savage, 1948), on the assumption that insurance can be conceptualized as a choice between acceptance either of a small probability of a large loss or of a certain small loss (the insurance premium). Recent research casts doubt upon this conceptualization by showing that *certain* losses are more attractive when framed as insurance premiums rather than monetary losses.

We first began thinking about this issue when we noticed that preference data presented in an early paper on prospect theory (Kahneman and Tversky, 1975) differed from results that we had obtained with similar preferences portrayed as insurance problems (Slovic and others, 1977). Specifically, Kahneman and Tversky presented people with a choice between a certain loss, such as $50, and a probability of losing a larger amount, such as a .25 chance to lose $200. For each pair of options, the expected loss from the gamble was equal to the certain loss from its alternative. Our study had used similar problems in the context of insurance and called the certain loss an insurance premium. Whereas Kahneman and Tversky's subjects preferred the gambles for moderate or high probabilities of loss, ours preferred the insurance.

Intrigued by this discrepancy, we decided to explore the effects of context (insurance versus preference) more systematically. Two situations were studied. In one, people were presented with a choice between accepting a .001 chance of losing $5,000 and a certain loss of $5; in the other, they were asked to choose between accepting a .25 chance of losing $200 and a certain loss of $50. The 208 subjects were paid volunteers who responded to an ad in a university newspaper. Each responded to only one problem situation (.001 or .25 chance of loss), which they initially received in only one context (insurance or preference). The results shown in Table 1 clearly indicate that the certain loss was more likely to be selected in the insurance as opposed to the preference context.

About one hour after the subjects had made these choices, they were presented again with the same problem, sometimes in the same context, some-

**Table 1. Proportions of Subjects Choosing the Certain Loss
in Insurance and Preference Contexts**

	Probability of Loss	
Context	.001	.25
Insurance	37/56	26/40
	66%	65%
Preference	28/72	8/40
	39%	20%

times in the other. When the context remained unchanged, so did choices: Only 5 percent of the subjects changed their responses. However, when the second problem was framed differently, 29 percent changed their responses. In 85 percent of the cases when subjects changed their responses, subjects chose the gamble in the preference setting and the insurance premium in the insurance setting. Moreover, people who first saw the problem in the preference context were three times more likely to change as just described than those who saw it first in the insurance context. This suggests that people are more likely to realize that an insurance premium implies a certain loss than they are to realize that a certain loss represents an insurance premium. Varying probabilities and losses in a more systematic way than we did, Schoemaker and Kunreuther (1979) and Hershey and Schoemaker (1980) have obtained similar context effects with a wide variety of problems.

What causes this strong context effect? One explanation is that paying an insurance premium is not psychologically equivalent to choosing a sure loss. The insurance context forces an individual to acknowledge that he or she is at risk. Paying a premium is an instrumental action that provides a benefit: It removes the risk; it buys safety. In contrast, accepting a certain loss is not perceived as saving one from an unattractive gamble. The logic of this interpretation is illustrated by the comments of a subject who chose the gamble in the preference condition and the premium in the insurance condition. When confronted with this inconsistency, the subject refused to change his preference, asserting that paying the premium seemed less aversive than choosing the certain loss. Asked whether he thought the preference and insurance problems were the same, he replied, "Yes, they're the same, but they look different."

A related interpretation is based on prospect theory, according to which one evaluates an option according to the change that it would make in one's position vis-à-vis some reference point. The theory asserts also (a) that losses are valued more heavily than gains of the same magnitude; (b) that the individual becomes increasingly less sensitive to a given change in outcome as the stakes get larger (that is, the value function is concave above the reference point and convex below it); (c) low-probability events tend to be given more weight than high-probability events, although special weight is given to events that are certain.

If the preference context is interpreted as a comparison between a gamble and a certain loss, the reference point is the individual's status quo. The gamble would seem less aversive than the certain loss, both because large losses are somewhat discounted in comparison to small losses (point b above) and because consequences that are certain to happen are given special weight (point c above).

In the insurance context, however, the reference point is loss of the premium. The choice is then between paying the premium or accepting the gamble. For example, consider paying a $50 premium to avoid a .25 chance of losing $200. Accepting the gamble provides a ¾ chance of gaining $50 (not paying the $50 premium and not losing on the gamble) and a ¼ chance of losing $150 (losing $200 on the gamble but saving the $50 premium). Because losses loom larger than gains and small probabilities tend to be overestimated, this gamble should be valued negatively; that is, it should seem less attractive than staying at the reference point of the insurance policy.

A third (and much simpler) explanation proposed by Kahneman and Tversky (1979) and by Hershey and Schoemaker (1980) is that the insurance context may trigger social norms about prudent behavior that are not associated with the preference context. The latter, they claim, may actually stimulate a gambling orientation.

If the interpretations proposed here are validated by further investigations, they would have important implications for insurance decision making and for protective behavior in general. The results suggest that people will be more likely to protect themselves from a probable hazard if they recognize that they are at risk and remain so unless they take protective action. Indeed, data from an extensive survey of people who did and did not insure themselves against flood or earthquake hazards support this notion (Kunreuther and others, 1978).

Response Mode, Framing, and Information Processing

The way in which an individual has to respond to the decision problem is an important aspect of framing. Although people are sometimes free to choose their response mode, more often some external source defines the problem either as one of judgment (evaluating individual options) or as one of choice (selecting one from two or more options). Many theories of decision making postulate an equivalence between judgment and choice. Such theories assume that each option X has a value $v(X)$ that determines its attractiveness in both contexts (for example, Luce, 1977). However, the descriptive validity of these theories is now in question. Much recent research has demonstrated that the information-processing strategies used prior to making choices are often quite different from the strategies employed in judging single options. As a result, choices and evaluative judgments of the same options often differ, sometimes dramatically. The conditions under which judgment and choice are similar or different need to be better understood (Einhorn and Hogarth, 1981).

Justification and Choice. One conception asserts that much of the deliberation prior to choice consists of finding a concise, coherent set of reasons that justify the selection of one option over the others. For example, Tversky (1972) provided evidence to support an elimination by aspects model of choice. According to this model, options are viewed as sets of aspects; that is, a car has a price, a model, a color, and so forth. At each stage in the choice process, one aspect is selected, with probability proportional to its importance. The options that are not adequate for each selected aspect are eliminated from the set of options considered at the following stage. Tversky argued that elimination by aspects is an appealing process because it is easy both to apply and to justify. It permits a choice to be resolved in a clear-cut fashion without reliance on relative weights, trade-off functions, or other numerical computations and eases demands on the decision maker's limited capacity for intuitive calculation.

Another example of justification processes comes from a study of difficult choices (Slovic, 1975). Each of two options was defined by two dimensions differing in importance. To maximize the difficulty of choice, these paired options were designed to have equal value by making the option that was superior on the more important dimension to be so inferior on the lesser dimension that its advantage was cancelled. The equating of options was done judgmentally. For example, one set of options involved gift packages with two components, cash and a coupon book offering miscellaneous products and services. The subject was shown two such gift packages with one component missing (see Table 2). The subject was asked to supply a value for the missing component large enough to make the two options equally attractive. Many different types of stimuli were used (for example, gift packages, pairs of jobs, routes to work), and the missing component was varied within each pair. Subjects were asked to equate various pairs of options and then to choose among them.

Contrary to the predictions of most choice theories, choices between these equally attractive alternatives were not made randomly. Rather, most subjects consistently selected the option that was superior on the more important dimension. For the example in Table 2, cash was generally viewed as more important than the coupon book, and, among pairs of equated gift packages, the option that offered more cash was selected 79 percent of the time. Apparently, reliance on the more important dimension makes a better justification ("I chose this gift package because it provided more cash") than random selection ("They looked about equally attractive, so I flipped a coin").

Table 2. A Typical Choice Pair

	Cash	Coupon Book Worth
Gift package A	$10	—
Gift package B	$20	$18

Source: Slovic, 1975.

Another demonstration of justification in choice comes from a study that presented college students and members of the League of Women Voters with both of the tasks shown in Figure 2 and Table 3 (Fischhoff, Slovic, and Lichtenstein, 1980).

In the first task (Table 3), subjects chose between a high variance and a low variance option involving the loss of life. In the second task, they were asked to evaluate three functions representing the way in which society should evaluate lives in multifatality situations. The instructions for the second task provided elaborate rationales for adopting each of the functional forms over a range between zero and one hundred lives lost in a single accident. Curve 1, the linear form, represents the view that every life lost is equally costly to society. Curve 2, the exponentially increasing function, represents the view that large losses of life are disproportionately serious; for example, that the loss of twenty lives is more than twice as bad as the loss of ten lives. Curve 3 represents a reduced sensitivity to large losses of life; for example, the loss of twenty lives is less than twice as bad as the loss of ten lives. Subjects were asked to study each curve and its rationale and then to indicate the ones with which they agreed most and least.

More than half of all subjects chose option A in task 1 (Table 3) and agreed most with curve 2 in task 2 (Figure 2). However, option A indicates a risk-seeking attitude toward loss of life, whereas curve 2 represents risk aversion. Choice of option A would be consistent with curve 3, which was the least favored view. These inconsistent results did not change appreciably when the degree of elaboration in the rationales given for the three curves was changed.

Subjects who were confronted with the inconsistency in their responses refused to change. They claimed to see no connection between the two tasks. Most appeared to be relying on some variant of this justification offered for choosing option A: "It would be immoral to allow the loss of forty lives or more when option A presents a good chance of coming out of the situation with no loss of life." This perspective was evoked by the structure of the choice problem but not by the task of evaluating the three functional relationships.

Because many theorists have proposed to use such choices as these to infer people's value functions (for example, Johnson and Huber, 1977; Raiffa, 1968), the results presented here may give cause for concern about this practice.

Anchoring and Adjustment. Just as choice problems trigger justification processes, single numerical judgments are prone to being influenced by anchoring and adjustment. In this process, a natural starting point is used as a first approximation or anchor for the judgment. This anchor is then adjusted to accommodate the implications of additional information. Often, the adjustment is smaller than it should be, considering the importance of the new information. An example of how anchoring can lead to strong differences between evaluation and choice comes from two experiments (Lichtenstein and Slovic, 1971, 1973), one of which was conducted on the floor of the Four Queens

Figure 2. Task 2: The Impact of Catastrophic Events*

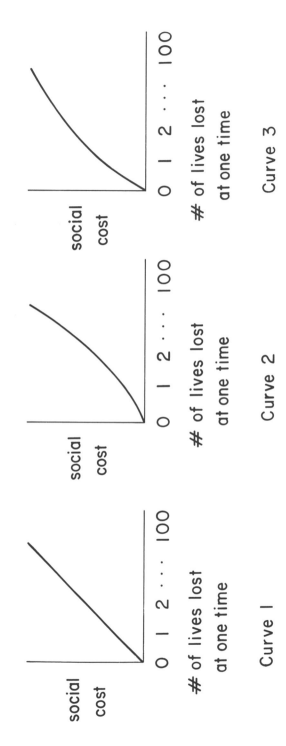

*Subjects were asked to rank the three proposals in order of preference.

Table 3. Task 1: Emergency Response

A committee in a large metropolitan area met recently to discuss contingency plans in the event of various emergencies. One emergency threat under consideration posed two options, both involving some loss of life. These are described below. Read them and indicate your opinion about the relative merits of each.

> Option A carries with it a .5 probability of containing the threat with a loss of 5 lives and a .5 probability of losing 95 lives. It is like taking the gamble: .5 lose 5 lives, .5 lose 95 lives.

> Option B carries with it a .5 probability of containing the threat with a loss of 40 lives and a .5 probability of losing 60 lives. It is like taking the gamble: .5 lose 40 lives, .5 lose 60 lives.

Which option would you select? Option A _____ Option B _____

Casino in Las Vegas. Consider the following pair of gambles used in the Las Vegas experiment: bet A: 11/12 chance to win 12 chips, and 1/12 chance to lose 24 chips; bet B: 2/12 chance to win 79 chips, and 10/12 chance to lose 5 chips, where the value of each chip was 25 cents. Notice that bet A had a much better chance of winning and that bet B offered a higher winning payoff. Subjects indicated, in two ways, the attractiveness of each bet in many such pairs. First, they made a simple choice, A or B. Later, they were asked to assume that they owned a ticket to play each bet, and they were to state the lowest price for which they would sell this ticket.

Presumably, both these selling prices and choices were governed by the same underlying factor, the attractiveness of each gamble. Therefore, subjects should have stated higher selling prices for the gambles that they preferred in the choice situation. In fact, subjects often chose one gamble yet stated a higher selling price for the other. For the particular pair of gambles just mentioned, bets A and B were chosen about equally often. However, bet B received a higher selling price about 88 percent of the time. Of the subjects who chose bet A, 87 percent gave a higher selling price to bet B, thus exhibiting an inconsistent preference pattern. Grether and Plott (1979), two skeptical economists, replicated this study with numerous variations designed to show that the observed inconsistencies were artifactual. They obtained essentially the same results as Lichtenstein and Slovic.

What accounts for this inconsistent pattern of preferences for gambles? Lichtenstein and Slovic concluded that subjects used different cognitive strategies when setting prices and making choices. Subjects often justified the choice of bet A in terms of its good odds, but they set a higher price for B because they anchored on its large winning payoff. For example, people who found a gamble basically attractive used the amount to win as a starting point. They then adjusted the amount to win downward to accommodate the less-than-perfect chance of winning and the fact that there was some amount to lose as well. Typically, this adjustment was small, and as a result, large winning payoffs caused people to set prices that were inconsistent with their choices.

Another way of looking at these results is in terms of the notion of compatibility. Because a selling price is expressed in terms of monetary units, subjects apparently found it easier to use the monetary aspects of the gamble to produce this type of response. Compatibility made the amount to win an anchor, which caused that aspect to dominate the response. Such bias did not exist with the choices, since each attribute of one gamble could be compared directly with the same attribute of the other. With no reason to use payoffs as a starting point, subjects were free to use other rules to determine (or to justify) their choices.

Compatibility Bias. A compatibility hypothesis was tested directly in a study by Slovic and MacPhillamy (1974). They predicted that dimensions common to each option in a choice situation would have greater influence than dimensions that were unique to a particular option. They asked subjects to compare pairs of students and to predict, on the basis of scores on two cue dimensions (tests), which student would get the higher college grade point average. One dimension was common to both students, while the other was unique. For example, student A might be described in terms of scores on tests of English skill and quantitative ability, whereas student B might be described by scores on tests of English skill and need for achievement.

In this example, the compatibility hypothesis implies that English skill will be weighted particularly heavily, because it is common to both students. The rationale is that a comparison between two students along the same dimension should be cognitively easier than a comparison between two students along different dimensions. The data strongly confirmed this hypothesis. Dimensions were weighted more heavily when common than when unique. After the experiment, most subjects indicated that they had not wanted to give more weight to the common dimension and that they were unaware of having done so.

There is, of course, no common dimension when students are judged one at a time; hence, one would expect a dimension that was common in choice to be given less weight in a judgment task. Evidence for this was also found. For example, consider student A, who scored 470 on English skill and 674 on quantitative ability and whose need-for-achievement score was missing. Twenty-four of 26 subjects gave student A a higher rating (that is, judgment) than student B, who had scored 566 on English and 474 on need for achievement, but whose quantitative score was missing. However, when choosing between students A and B, ten subjects who had given a higher rating to student A chose B but only two reversed in the other direction. Many other such differences between judgment and choice can be found in Slovic and MacPhillamy's (1974) data.

Implications for Risk Assessment

The message of this research is that the amalgamation of different types of information and values in an overall judgment or decision is a difficult cognitive process. Even when all factors are known and made explicit, subtle aspects of problem formulation, acting in combination with our intellectual predispositions and limitations, affect the balance that we strike among them. These effects seem endemic to a wide range of behaviors. Here, we discuss briefly their implications for two important components of risk assessment.

Eliciting Labile Values. Value judgments indicating the desired trade-offs between important decision outcomes lie at the heart of individual and societal risk assessment. For example, a person considering either surgery or radiation therapy as treatment for lung cancer must balance the enhanced life expectancy that surgery confers against the greater risk of sudden death that it entails (MacNeil, Weichselbaum, and Pauker, 1978). The evaluation that society makes of different energy technologies can be guided, in part, by whether it decides to give particularly great weight to potentially catastrophic accidents. Many observers advocate making such values explicit in order to help individuals and society to make better decisions. Some observers call for direct elicitation of values through surveys, hearings, and the like, whereas others prefer to infer values from the preferences revealed by actual decisions. Both approaches assume that people know their own values and that elicitation methods are unbiased channels that translate subjective feelings into analytically usable expressions.

We doubt these assumptions. First, decision problems with high stakes tend to be unique and unfamiliar. They take us into situations in which we have never thought through the implications of values and beliefs acquired in simpler, more familiar settings. Second, due to the strong effects of framing and to information-processing considerations, elicitation procedures become major forces in shaping the expression of values, especially when such values are ill-defined (Fischhoff, Slovic, and Lichtenstein, 1980). In such cases, the method becomes the message. Subtle aspects of how problems are posed, questions are phrased, and responses are elicited can have substantial impact on judgments that supposedly express people's preferences.

One could hope that further research and analysis would identify better ways to ask questions about values. Although some methods distort values and should be avoided, others educate and deepen the respondent's perspectives. If we are interested in what people really feel about a value issue, there may be no substitute for an interactive elicitation procedure, one that employs multiple methods and acknowledges the elicitor's role in helping the respondent to create and enunciate values.

Informing People About Risk. One dramatic change in recent years is growing public awareness of the risks encountered in daily experience. Radiation hazards, medicinal side effects, occupational disease, food contaminants, toxic chemicals, and mechanical malfunctions increasingly seem to fill our newspapers and our thoughts. A consequence of this growing awareness has been pressure on designers and regulators of hazardous enterprises to inform people about the risks that they face (Morris, Mazis, and Barofsky, 1980; Slovic, Fischhoff, and Lichtenstein, 1980).

Clearly, better information about risk is crucial to making better personal decisions and to participating more effectively in the political processes whereby societal standards are developed and enforced. Despite good intentions, however, it may be quite difficult to create effective informational programs. Doing an adequate job means finding cogent ways of presenting complex, technical material that is clouded by uncertainty and subject to distortion by the listener's preconceptions — or misconceptions — about the hazard and its consequences. Moreover, as we have seen, people are often at the mercy of the way in which problems are formulated. Those responsible for determining the content and format of information programs thus have considerable ability to manipulate perceptions. Moreover, since these effects are not widely known, people may inadvertently be manipulating their own perceptions by casual decisions they make about how to organize their knowledge.

The stakes in risk problems are high — product viability, jobs, energy costs, willingness of patients to accept treatments, public safety and health, and so forth. Potential conflicts of interest abound. When subtle aspects of how (or what) information is presented make a significant difference in people's responses, one needs to determine the formulation that should be used. Making that decision takes one out of psychology and into the domains of law, ethics, and politics.

References

Einhorn, H. J., and Hogarth, R. M. "Behavioral Decision Theory: Processes of Judgment and Choice." *Annual Review of Psychology,* 1981, *32,* 53–88.

Fischhoff, B., Slovic, P., and Lichtenstein, S. "Fault Trees: Sensitivity of Estimated Failure Probabilities to Problem Representation." *Journal of Experimental Psychology: Human Perception and Performance,* 1978, *4,* 330–344.

Fischhoff, B., Slovic, P., and Lichtenstein, S. "Knowing What You Want: Measuring Labile Values." In T. Wallsten (Ed.), *Cognitive Processes in Choice and Decision Behavior.* Hillsdale, N.J.: Erlbaum, 1980.

Friedman, M., and Savage, L. J. "The Utility Analysis of Choices Involving Risk." *Journal of Political Economy,* 1948, *56,* 279–304.

Grether, D. M., and Plott, C. R. "Economic Theory of Choice and the Preference Reversal Phenomenon." *American Economic Review,* 1979, *69,* 623–638.

Hershey, J. C., and Schoemaker, P. J. H. "Risk Taking and Problem Context in the Domain of Losses: An Expected-Utility Analysis." *The Journal of Risk and Insurance,* 1980, *47,* 111–132.

Johnson, E. M., and Huber, G. P. "The Technology of Utility Assessment." *IEEE Transactions on Systems, Man, and Cybernetics,* 1977, *SMC-7,* 311–325.

Kahneman, D., and Tversky, A. "Value Theory: An Analysis of Choices Under Risk." Paper presented at a conference on public economics, Jerusalem, Israel, June 1975.

Kahneman, D., and Tversky, A. "Prospect Theory: An Analysis of Decisions Under Risk." *Econometrica*, 1979, *47*, 262–291.

Kunreuther, H. C., and others. *Disaster Insurance Protection: Public Policy Lessons.* New York: Wiley, 1978.

Lichtenstein, S., and Slovic, P. "Reversals of Preference Between Bids and Choices in Gambling Decisions." *Journal of Experimental Psychology*, 1971, *89*, 46–55.

Lichtenstein, S., and Slovic, P. "Response-Induced Reversals of Preference in Gambling: An Extended Replication in Las Vegas." *Journal of Experimental Psychology*, 1973, *101*, 16–20.

Luce, R. D. "The Choice Axiom After Twenty Years." *Journal of Mathematical Psychology*, 1977, *15*, 215–233.

MacNeil, B. J., Weichselbaum, R., and Pauker, S. G. "Fallacy of the Five Year Survival in Lung Cancer." *New England Journal of Medicine*, 1978, *299*, 1397–1401.

Morris, L., Mazis, M., and Barofsky, I. (Eds.). *Product Labeling and Health Risks.* Banbury Report 6. Cold Spring Harbor, N.Y.: Cold Spring Harbor Laboratory, 1980.

Payne, J. W., and Braunstein, M. L. "Preferences Among Gambles with Equal Underlying Distributions." *Journal of Experimental Psychology*, 1971, *87*, 13–18.

Raiffa, H. *Decision Analysis: Introductory Lectures on Choice Under Uncertainty.* Reading, Mass.: Addison-Wesley, 1968.

Robertson, L. S. "The Great Seat Belt Campaign Flop." *Journal of Communication*, 1976, *26*, 41–45.

Schoemaker, P. J. H., and Kunreuther, H. C. "An Experimental Study of Insurance Decisions." *Journal of Risk and Insurance*, 1979, *46*, 603–618.

Slovic, P. "From Shakespeare to Simon: Speculations—and Some Evidence—About Man's Ability to Process Information." *ORI Research Monograph*, 1972, *12*, (2).

Slovic, P. "Choice Between Equally Valued Alternatives." *Journal of Experimental Psychology: Human Perception and Performance,*, 1975, *1*, 280–287.

Slovic, P., Fischhoff, B., and Lichtenstein, S. "Accident Probabilties and Seat Belt Usage: A Psychological Perspective." *Accident Analysis and Prevention*, 1978, *10*, 281–285.

Slovic, P., Fischhoff, B., and Lichtenstein, S. "Informing People About Risk." In L. Morris, M. Mazis, and I. Barofsky (Eds.), *Product Labeling and Health Risks.* Banbury Report 6. Cold Spring Harbor, N.Y.: Cold Spring Harbor Laboratory, 1980.

Slovic, P., Fischhoff, B., Lichtenstein, S., Corrigan, B., and Combs, B. "Preference for Insuring Against Probable Small Losses: Implications for the Theory and Practice of Insurance." *Journal of Risk and Insurance*, 1977, *44*, 237–258.

Slovic, P., and Lichtenstein, S. "The Importance of Variance Preferences in Gambling Decisions." *Journal of Experimental Psychology*, 1968, *78*, 646–654.

Slovic, P., and MacPhillamy, D. J. "Dimensional Commensurability and Cue Utilization in Comparative Judgment." *Organizational Behavior and Human Performance*, 1974, *11*, 172–194.

Tversky, A. "Elimination by Aspects: A Theory of Choice." *Psychological Review*, 1972, *79*, 281–299.

Paul Slovic, Baruch Fischhoff, and Sarah Lichtenstein
are research associates at Decision Research, a branch of
Perceptronics, 1201 Oak Street, Eugene, Oregon 97401.

When faced with a dilemma, seek the right question.

The Problem of the Problem

J. W. Getzels

"The formulation of a problem," said Albert Einstein (Einstein and Infeld, 1938), "if often more essential than its solution, which may be merely a matter of mathematical or experimental skill. To raise new questions, new possibilities, to regard old questions from a new angle, requires creative imagination and marks real advance in science" (p. 92).

This is true not only in science but in all activities calling for thought. Max Wertheimer (1945) generalized Einstein's point as follows: "The function of thinking is not just solving an actual problem but discovering, envisaging, going into deeper questions. Often in great discoveries the most important thing is that a certain question is found. Envisaging, putting the productive question is often a more important, often a greater achievement than the solution of a set question" (p. 123).

Need questions be found? Is not the world already teeming with problems and dilemmas at home and in business, in economics and education, in art and in science, and in fact wherever we look, including into ourselves? The world is, of course, teeming with conflicts and dilemmas. But the conflicts and dilemmas do not present themselves automatically as problems capable of res-

Portions of this chapter are drawn from previously published work (for example, Getzels, 1964, 1975, 1979, 1980; Getzels and Csikszentmihalyi, 1967, 1976). I thank Professor Mihaly Csikszentmihalyi for the use of collaborative material; I also thank Professor R. Bruce McPherson for providing the interviews with administrators.

R. Hogarth (Ed.). *New Directions for Methodology of Social and Behavioral Science: Question Framing and Response Consistency,* no. 11. San Francisco: Jossey-Bass, March 1982.

olution or even of sensible contemplation. They must be specified and formulated in fruitful and often radical ways if they are to be moved toward productive termination.

Henry Moore (1955) describes the process of problem finding in art in these words: "I sometimes begin drawing with no preconceived problem to solve, with only a desire to use pencil on paper and only make lines, tones, and styles with no conscious aim. But as my mind takes in what is so produced, a point arrives where some idea becomes conscious and crystallizes, and then control and ordering begin to take place" (p. 77).

What Moore is describing is the finding and formulating of a problem. Prior to its emergence, there is no structure and no task; there is nothing to solve. After the problem is posed, the skill of the artist takes over; control and ordering begin. The crucial step is how the formless situation where there is no problem (or there is only an indeterminate dilemma where the problem is moot) is transformed into a situation where a problem — in this case, a creative problem — emerges for solution. The question that is asked is the forerunner of the quality of the solution that will be attained. Transforming the dilemma into a fruitful problem — putting the right question, as the saying goes — may be no less an intellectual achievement than attaining the effective solution once the productive problem is posed.

The same dilemma may give rise to the formulation of diverse and even contradictory problems — problems that lead to different and sometimes opposite lines of inquiry and resolution. This is the case not only in imaginative art, where presumably anything goes, but in the so-called exact sciences. Consider as one illustration this report of a recent advance in medical research in leukemia: "Perhaps the most remarkable progress has been made by a group of researchers lead by Professor Leo Sachs. . . . Somehow in leukemia the body becomes infected by cells that refuse to age and die naturally the way normal healthy cells do. These harmful cells thus remain trapped in a perpetual state of youth. Current treatment tries to kill these hostile cells by poisoning them. Unfortunately, the drugs are so toxic, they usually also kill the perfectly healthy cells, often causing death by the potent side effects. *So Professor Sachs posed a new question. Would it be possible to find a drug that would make the leukemic cells mature and simply die?* Professor Sachs's fresh approach was soon to pay dividends in opening a wide range of previously unforeseen possibilities" (Griver, 1979, p. 7). The first formulation of the problem led to seeking a poison to kill the infected cells as the resolution of the dilemma; the second, to seeking an elixir to vivify the infected cells.

Consider, finally, the following situation as paradigmatic of the crucial distinction between dilemma and problem and of the relation between the quality of the problem that is formulated and the quality of the solution that is attained: An automobile is traveling on a deserted country road and blows a tire. The occupants of the automobile go to the trunk and discover that there is no jack. They define their dilemma by posing the problem: "Where can we get a jack?" They look about, see some empty barns but no habitation, and recall that, several miles back they had passed a service station. They decide to walk back to the station to get a jack. While they are gone, an automobile coming from the other direction also blows a tire. The occupants of this automobile go to the trunk and discover that there is no jack. They define their dilemma by posing the problem: "How can we raise the automobile?" They look about and see, adjacent to the road, a barn with a pulley for lifting bales of hay to the loft. They move the automobile to the barn, raise it on the pulley, change the tire, and drive off, while the occupants of the first car are still trudging toward the service station.

The casual comment could be, "What a clever solution!" The more fundamental observation would be, "What a clever question!" For the quality of the solution that was attained was a function of the quality of the question that was formulated. The same dilemma faced the occupants of both cars, but those in the first car transformed the dilemma into the problem of getting a jack, which led to one course of action. Those in the second car transformed the same dilemma into a different problem, that of raising the car, which pointed to another course of action. And this—finding and formulating the problem—made all the difference in the quality of the solutions that were reached by the two groups to the identical dilemma.

Despite the manifest role of problems in initiating thought and the function that new problems have in guiding thought toward new solutions, very little is known about how problems are found and formulated. Although there are numerous theoretical statements, a plethora of psychometric instruments, and quite literally thousands of empirical studies on problem solving (that is, on the problem of the solution), there is hardly any work of a similar nature on problem posing or what might be called the problem of the problem.

The assumption seems to have been that only answers and solutions count and that only their attainment requires thought and deserves empirical study. To cite one example, although the journal *Cognitive Science* informs potential contributors that it publishes articles "on such topics as the representation of knowledge, language processing, image processing, question answering, inference, learning, problem solving, and planning" (see "Information to Authors"), it characteristically fails to mention question asking or problem posing, as if questions and problems could be picked up at will. The consequence has been that little conceptual attention (De Bono, 1978; Dewey, 1933; Reitman, 1965) and less empirical inquiry have been directed to the meaning and variety of problems. With the exception of the studies to be sketched here, there has been hardly any systematic exploration of the process of finding and formulating problems, that is, of the problem of the problem.

Problems: Presented, Discovered, Created

At first glance, it does not seem sensible to raise a question about what is meant by a problem. We have faced problems since our earliest days, and there is almost no one who does not have a problem. The term is so familiar that, even in the large technical literature on problem solving, it is ordinarily taken for granted that everyone knows what is meant by a problem.

When the term is dealt with at all, it is usually defined so as to conform to what presumably everyone already knows. Thus, Norman R. F. Maier (1970) says, "A problem exists when a response to a given situation is blocked" (p. 203). Similarly, Karl Duncker (1945) says, "A problem arises when a living creature has a goal but does not know how the goal is to be reached" (p. 1). Recently, McDermott (1978) put it simply: "A problem is just a difficult action" (p. 71).

This seems reasonable enough: A problem is a difficulty, an obstacle to a goal. Yet, somehow this description does not quite fit what Einstein and Wertheimer were referring to or what Moore and the leukemia researchers seemed to mean by a problem. It is surely not what Dewey (1938) was referring to when he said, "A problem represents a partial transformation of a problematic situation into a determinate situation" (p. 108). Nor is it what *Webster's* (1968) means when it says that a problem is "a question raised or to be raised for inquiry, consideration, discussion, decision, or solution" (p. 1807). Here, as in the case of the scientist who seeks a problem to work on or the artist who constructs a still-life problem, the problem is not an obstacle but in a very real sense the goal itself.

To realize the different—indeed, the contradictory—phenomena that can be subsumed under the single term *problem,* one need only compare two definitions: "A problem exists when a response to a given situation is blocked," and a problem is "a question raised or to be raised for inquiry." At one extreme, the word *problem* can refer to an undesired situation that one wishes to avoid or mitigate; at the other, it can refer to a desirable situation that one strives to find or create. It is no contradiction for the graduate student who seeks a dissertation topic to say that his or her problem is to find a problem.

It is possible to classify problems by three factors: whether the problem already exists, who propounds it, and whether it has a known formulation, a known method of solution, or a known solution. From this point of view, ten types of problems can be identified:

1. The problem is given (is known) and there is a standard method for solving it, known to the would-be problem solver (for example, experimental subject, student) and to others (for example, experimenter, teacher), guaranteeing a solution in a finite number of steps.

2. The problem is given but no method for solving it is known to the problem solver, although it is known to others.

3. The problem is given but no method for solving it is known to the problem solver or to others.

4. The problem itself exists but remains to be identified (become known) by the problem solver, although it is known to others.

5. The problem exists but remains to be identified by the problem solver and by the others.

6. The problem exists but remains to be identified (as in 4 and 5) and there is a standard method for solving it, once the problem is discovered known to the problem solver and to the others (as in 1).

7. The problem exists but remains to be identified, and no standard method for solving it is known to the problem solver, although known to others (as in 2).

8. The problem exists but remains to be identified, and no method for solving it is known to the problem solver or to others (as in 3).

9. The problem does not yet exist but is invented or conceived, and a method for solving it is known or becomes known once the problem is formulated.

10. The problem does not yet exist but is invented or conceived, and a method for solving it is not known (Libby, n.d.).

This typology does not, of course, exhaust the possibilities. However, enough has been said to suggest the principle of a wide variety of problems and the heuristic value of differentiating among them. For present purposes, it will suffice to distinguish three classes of problem situation: presented problem situations, discovered problem situations, and created problem situations.

In a presented problem situation — or, to be precise, in one instance of it — the problem exists, and it is propounded to the problem solver. A teacher teaches that the area of a rectangle is side *a* times side *b,* and the pupil is required to solve the problem: What is the area of a rectangle when *a* is 3 and *b* is 4? Here, the problem is given — it is presented — and in the particular instance, it has a known formulation, a known method of solution, and a solution known to others if not yet to the problem solver.

Consider now the discovered problem situation — or, again, one instance of it. Here, the problem also exists, but it is discovered by oneself rather than propounded by another, and it may or may not have a known formulation, known method of solution, or known solution. Roentgen saw a fogged photographic plate as others had before him, but, while the others had seen it only as a nuisance, he asked, "Why is the plate fogged?" — a self-initiated problem that led to the discovery of the X ray and a revolution in atomic science. Here, the problem was not presented to the problem solver by another; he discovered the problem himself and even took pleasure in doing so. This is clearly different from the presented problem situation.

Consider, finally, the created problem situation. Here, the problem does not exist until someone invents or creates it. Maier invents a series of problems to test problem-solving abilities. The scientist conceives of the problem of investigating the nature and speed of light. The artist creates a still-life problem where no such problem existed before. It makes no sense to think of these situations as obstacles that one meets through accident, misfortune, ignorance, or ineptitude. Quite the contrary; these are situations that one strives to formulate and bring into being. Indeed, a well-formulated problem is at once the result of knowledge, a stimulus to more knowledge, and, most important, knowledge itself (Henle, 1971). In Polanyi's (1958) words: "To see a problem is a definite addition to knowledge, as much as it is to see a tree, or to see a mathematical proof—or a joke. . . . To recognize a problem which can be solved and is worth solving is in fact a discovery in its own right" (p. 120).

The portion of human activity that is held in highest esteem—pure science, fine art, technological invention, systematic philosophy—is devoted as much to discovering, creating, and formulating problems as it is to solving them. This behavior is not undertaken only in order to overcome obstacles because they are a threat to personal well-being; often, the problems are sought out even at the cost of well-being, sometimes at the risk of life itself.

Galileo raised questions about the accepted cosmology of his time despite the threat of being burned at the stake for it. Matisse set himself the problem of painting grass red and roses green despite the derision of the public and established artists, who called him a wild beast. Geneticists persisted in posing the problem of what would happen if one genetic stuff were combined with another, as in recombinant DNA, despite the possibility of a catastrophic outcome. At a different level, perhaps most remarkable of all, a four-year-old asks spontaneously, "Why does it get lighter outside when we put the light out inside?" (Henle, 1971, p. 123) and enjoys the problem he has posed, as in fact he has a right to.

As Bunge (1967, pp. 165–167) points out, all animals have the capacity for taking notice of problems as obstacles to a goal; machines, too, can be programmed to sense problems as obstacles. But, as human beings, we not only sense problems as obstacles standing in our way but also go out of our way to discover and create new problems. We are not only problem solvers but also problem finders, "problemizing" beings who, besides solving the problems posed by our natural and social habitats, feel a need for and pleasure in posing problems.

From the earliest wonder and play of the child to the highest advances of art and science, this engagement of human beings with the problematic makes human thought uniquely human. The deeper the problems found, posed, and ultimately solved, the greater the human achievement. Put in the terms of our taxonomy, the production of discovered or created problems is often a more significant accomplishment than the production of solutions to presented problems. It is in this sense that the concentration of empirical inquiry on the problem of the solution and the concurrent neglect of the problem of the problem are so puzzling.

Investigating the Created Problem

Over a period of some years, a number of colleagues and students and I have been attempting to investigate the nature of problems and the process of finding and formulating them. We began with problem posing in art along lines raised by Moore's account, and we proceeded to more ordinary problems, including problems in cognition and interpersonal relations.

The first study was part of a longitudinal investigation of creative thinking, using students from the School of the Art Institute of Chicago (Getzels and Csikszentmihalyi, 1976). We began in the usual psychological mode by administering a variety of biographical, perceptual, cognitive, and personality instruments, comparing the responses of the art students with the responses of other students, and correlating the observations with grade point averages in studio courses and with other criteria of creative performance.

Initially, we were exhilarated by the results. We found significant differences in character between the art students and the other students and significant correlations between the characteristics of the art students and their creative performance. As an instance, the correlation between low economic values on the Allport-Vernon-Lindzey Study of Values and the grade point average of male fine art students in studio courses was .47.

But when the first exhilaration was over and we stepped back to survey the results, we were struck by the thought that we had not come much closer to understanding, or even describing, creative production. We knew something more about the correlates of creative performance than we did when we started, but we knew nothing much more about our own problem, the processes underlying creative performance. To be sure, there was a .47 correlation between values and creative achievement, but what did that say about the way in which creative achievement was attained?

Instead of observing how a creative solution or imaginative work was achieved starting with its inception as a dilemma or problem and concluding with its outcome as a product, we had fallen into the familiar trap of correlating a readily obtainable independent variable (in this case, a personal characteristic) with an already available dependent variable (in this case, a grade point average). If we were to explore creative thinking in art, which was our intent, it remained necessary to observe how the creative product — a drawing or painting, say — was achieved, from the beginning to the conclusion, and how the quality of the process was related to the quality of the product.

Our initial observations and conversations with the artists as they worked at their easels were fascinating but bewildering. Some artists worked impulsively; others, reflectively. Some artists daubed flecks of color on the canvas with a brush, while others smeared heavy smudges of paint with a trowel. One artist said that he painted because it was the only thing he could do; another, because he wanted to develop a new vision of man. Nothing we saw or heard was related to the creative quality of the product. However — and this was crucial — we also observed that students in advertising or industrial art ordinarily began with a specific assignment, a problem as specific as drawing an illustration for a cornflake box, while students in fine art usually began with only a blank canvas before them; they had to find or create the problem that they were to work on themselves. In effect, advertising or industrial artists work in the context of presented problems, while fine artists work in the context of discovered or created problems.

The investigation made evident phenomenally what had been proposed conceptually, namely, that problem posing is a critical phase of the creative thought process. It was imperative to observe not only how an artistic problem is worked on toward solution but also how the artistic problem, to repeat Wertheimer's term, is *found.*

To observe how one solves a problem, we administer one or more of the numerous standard instruments and methods devised for this purpose (the Kohs Blocks, the Vygotsky, Piaget's tasks, or the Wechsler or Binet), watch the performance, and draw inferences about the process and quality of the problem solving from what is done and what is said. But, suppose we want to observe how one finds a problem—how one discovers, invents, poses, or formulates a problem. What can be done? We searched diligently, but we were unable to locate any standard instruments or methods, so we had to devise a way of observing and evaluating the phenomena of problem finding just as ways had to be devised for problem solving.

Once we formulated our problem in these terms, a procedure suggested itself. We furnished a studio at the Art Institute school with two tables, an easel, a drawing board, paper, and a variety of dry media. On one table, we placed a collection of some thirty objects used at the school to construct still-life problems. Then, we asked thirty-one fine arts students to use one or more of the objects on the first table to create a still-life problem on the second table and to produce a drawing of the still-life problem that they had created.

We observed what they did in creating the still-life problem and in producing the drawing, and we interviewed them about what they had done and how they felt in the situation. In this way, we were able to differentiate the process of problem finding among thirty-one artists along a number of dimensions—for example, the number or breadth of objects examined, the depth of exploration of each object, the uniqueness of the objects used. The procedure for examining the central issue, namely, the relation between the quality of the problem finding and the quality of the completed drawing, was quite simple. We ranked the thirty-one artists on the quality of their problem finding before they began the actual drawing, arranged an exhibition of finished drawings, and asked five recognized artist critics who had served in a similar capacity in real exhibitions to rank the drawings on their quality as original work. The relation between the two sets of rankings was significantly positive; to be precise, the correlation was .54.

The full details of the investigation are given elsewhere (Getzels and Csikszentmihalyi, 1976). No more will be said about it here, except for a word about the longitudinal phase. Five to six years after the students had graduated from art school—that is, about seven years after the problem-posing observations were made—we correlated these rankings with the relative success of the former students as professional artists. The correlation was .30, significant at the .05 level. When two other ratings of problem formulation (one collected during the drawing stage, the other by interview) were added to pre-drawing ratings, the correlation rose to .41.

The results of this study were so encouraging that the model was applied in a variety of more common contexts, including cognition, interpersonal relations, students' perception of school problems, and, more recently, the role of problem formulation in administrative decision making. Only the first four studies can be dealt with here.

Patricia Arlin (1974) showed that the differential formulation of problems is not an aberrant variable; instead, it is systematically related to other aspects of human thought: The higher the stage of cognitive development in Piaget's terms, the higher the quality of the problem that is formulated. Donald Schwartz (1974) moved the inquiry from artistic and cognitive to social and affective aspects of behavior. He showed that the same interpersonal dilemma is transformed by some individuals into one problem and by other individuals into another problem. Further, there is a hierarchy of formulations, ranging from egocentric to socially sensitive problems. That is, some individuals consistently formulate interpersonal dilemmas as problems from their own point of view, and other individuals consistently formulate the same dilemmas as problems that take the points of view of the other person involved into account. Jonathan Smilansky (1977) investigated the content of problems perceived by students in characteristic school dilemmas and the form in which the problems were articulated. Not only did the content of the problems vary but, what was more important, the form in which the problems were put could vary, even when the content was the same. It ranged from egocentric formulations at one extreme to socially sensitive formulations at the other. There were systematic relations between the content and form of the problems and certain personal characteristics of those who were formulating the problems.

A study still in progress is investigating how administrative dilemmas are formulated as problems for decision (see Getzels, 1980). Although one must beware of analogies, the processes often seem very close to those observed in the preceding studies and to the paradigmatic instance of the dilemma of the flat tire, which was formulated as different problems that led to different policies and courses of action.

Asked to describe a difficult decision that he had to make, one superintendent of schools gave this account: One school in his district had become overcrowded, and the larger building to replace it would not be completed for two years. In the meantime, seventeen mobile classrooms filled the playground and the parking lot, but they were insufficient for the expected influx of children in the fall.

The dilemma was obvious—overcrowding. Discussion among the principal, superintendent, and president of the board of education centered on two problems: whether to get more mobile classrooms and where to put them, or whether to move the excess children to other, less crowded schools and how to transport them there. Typically, one dilemma was transformed into two different problems. The decision was left up to the superintendent, and it was to depend on the problem that lent itself to the easiest solution. As the superintendent tells it, in due course it occurred to him that the problem was really not whether to get more mobile classrooms and where to put them or whether to get rid of the excess children and how to transport them, but simply how to get more space.

Once this problem was formulated, the solution proved not at all difficult. It was possible to build a temporary classroom structure that could later be converted to commercial use, and this is what was done. The similarity of this situation to the paradigmatic instance is self-evident: Get a jack or raise the car; more mobile classrooms or more space!

Although it seems more normal to go from a dilemma to formulating a problem for solution, the interviews revealed that the administrator must often proceed in the opposite direction, following an already formulated problem brought to him for solution back to the dilemma that someone else had transformed into the problem that the administrator is required to solve.

A number of administrators said that this in fact might be the more common circumstance; surely, it was the more difficult one. Once someone has transformed a dilemma into a problem, it is hard (or even impossible) for him to perceive the dilemma as any other problem; a solution that is not responsive to the problem as already formulated is either no solution or the wrong solution. One principal gives this account: One of her teachers came to the office and said, "Johnny has been disruptive again, and he is old enough now to be expelled. How shall we go about expelling him?" The principal responded, "Yes, I know Johnny has been a nuisance. But maybe the question is, how can we go about getting him some help for what is troubling him again?" In the principal's words, "The teacher flounced out of my office into the teachers' lounge and announced, 'Whenever I go to that women with a real problem to be taken care of, she never does anything about it.'"

An unanticipated but surprisingly common issue regarding dilemmas, problems, and decisions was brought to light by these interviews. Not one administrator did not try to articulate the experience that some of the most critical decisions that he had had to make came in response to manifest problems that may have had ulterior latent purposes. That is, underlying the apparent problem with which the administrator is confronted and that he is asked to solve, there may be a covert meaning that he must recognize if the fundamental dilemma is to be dealt with effectively.

A superintendent gives the following account: One new teacher had a reputation for being a superb instructor but abrasive in relations with administrators. On the first day of school, a half-hour before the first period, the teacher walked into the principal's office and made a request: "I like to sit on a high stool when I teach. Could you get one for me?" On its face, this seemed like an absurd request to make in the tumult of a new school year.

Yet, the principal was quite sure later that if he had reacted only to the manifest problem, which at first he had been tempted to do, he would have made a serious mistake. He decided instead that, consciously or unconsciously, the teacher was testing the new teacher-administrator relationship: Would the new administrator be like all the others, or would the teacher receive assistance, even if the request seemed eccentric? The principal secured a stool in time for the teacher's first class, and during his entire tenure at the school, the teacher who had been abrasive was the principal's staunchest supporter.

There are latent meanings and unspoken purposes behind a great many of the manifest problems brought to administrators: a test, as in the present case; an excuse to establish contact; an appeal for help with a personal dilemma. Little is known about the symbolism of the problems presented to administrators, which, like slips of the tongue or apparent accidents, can represent dilemmas whose problems remain to be discovered.

Conclusion

Before we conclude, it will be necessary to spell out several caveats. Problems and solutions are not as discontinuous as the necessarily schematic account presented here may have implied. They meld into one another, and the problem can be altered in the very process of solution; to emphasize the formulation of problems is not to diminish the importance of their solution. With respect to the observations of how the problems were formulated, as in the observation of how problems are solved, it was assumed that the observable behavior and the inferred underlying processes are in some wise isomorphic. And, of course, despite assurances from the majority of those whom we observed that their behavior under observation did not differ from their behavior in the usual situation, it must not be forgotten that the observations depended on experiments, questionnaires, and interviews, with their unavoidable constraints.

Nonetheless, allowing even for these caveats, a number of things may be said with some assurance, or at least they can be posed as reasonable issues for further inquiry. The discovery and formulation of problems can be studied empirically. There are individual differences in the discovery and formulation of problems as there are in the attainment of solutions to problems that have already been formulated. There is a positive relation between the quality of a problem that is found and the quality of the solution that is attained. Perhaps most importantly, the problem of the problem is well worth investigating not only as an addendum to problem solving, which is typically what has been done when it was done at all, but as a fruitful conceptual and empirical issue in its own right.

The difference between the imaginative scholar and the pedant is not that the one is better informed than the other—quite often, the contrary is the case. Nor is the difference between the creative scientist and the technician

·that the one is more methodologically proficient than the other—again, quite often, the contrary is the case. The difference between the original artist and the copyist is not that the one is a more skilled craftsman than the other—here, too, the contrary is quite often the case.

Rather, it seems that the one (the pedant, the technician, the copyist) is content or able only to apply his knowledge, skill, or talent to situations where the problems have already been formulated, while the other (the scholar, the scientist, the artist) is impelled and able to apply his knowledge, skill, or talent to situations in which he himself must find and formulate the problem. To return to the taxonomy sketched earlier, the former works in the context of presented problem situations; the latter, in the context of discovered or created problem situations.

At the root of an answer is a question. At the core of an effective solution is a productive problem. It is this that makes the problem of the problem such an important subject for systematic inquiry. In describing what impels the creative scientist, Albert Einstein (Einstein and Infeld, 1938) made this distinction between a scientist and a detective, although both seek solutions to problems: "For the detective, the crime is given, the problem posed: Who killed Cock Robin? The scientist must at least in part commit his own crime" (p. 76). Gertrude Stein made the same point more generally, albeit more obliquely: "The whole question of questions and not answers is very interesting. Suppose no one asked a question. What would the answer be?"

References

Arlin, P. K. "Problem Finding: The Relation Between Cognitive Process Variables and Problem-Finding Performance." Unpublished doctoral dissertation, University of Chicago, 1974.

Bunge, M. *Scientific Research I: The Search for System.* New York: Springer-Verlag, 1967.

De Bono, E. *Opportunities.* London: Associated Business Programmes, 1978.

Dewey, J. *How We Think.* New York: D. C. Heath, 1933.

Dewey, J. *Logic: The Theory of Inquiry.* New York: Henry Holt, 1938.

Duncker, K. "On Problem Solving." *Psychological Monographs,* 1945, *58* (5) (entire issue).

Einstein, A., and Infeld, L. *The Evolution of Physics.* New York: Simon & Schuster, 1938.

Getzels, J. W. "Creative Thinking, Problem Solving, and Instruction." In E. R. Hilgard (Ed.), *Theories of Learning and Instruction.* The 63rd yearbook of the National Society for the Study of Education, Part I. Chicago: University of Chicago Press, 1964.

Getzels, J. W. "Problem Finding and the Inventiveness of Solution." *Journal of Creative Behavior,* 1975, *9,* 12–18.

Getzels, J. W. "Problem Finding: A Theoretical Note." *Cognitive Science,* 1979, *3,* 167–172.

Getzels, J. W. "Alternative Directions for Research in Educational Administration." In R. H. Farquhar and I. E. Housego (Eds.), *Canadian and Comparative Educational Administration.* Vancouver: Educational Extension, University of British Columbia, 1980.

Getzels, J. W., and Csikszentmihalyi, M. "Scientific Creativity." *Science Journal,* 1967, *3,* 80–84.

Getzels, J. W., and Csikszentmihalyi, M. *The Creative Vision: A Longitudinal Study of Problem Finding in Art.* New York: Wiley, 1976.

Griver, S. "Coming Close to Curing Leukemia." *Israel Digest,* 1979, *22,* 7.

Henle, M. "The Snail Beneath the Shell." *Abraxas,* 1971, *1,* 119–133.

Libby, W. L. "Tools for Discovery of Problems and Their Solutions (Heuristics)." Unpublished paper, Center for Programs in Government Administration, University of Chicago, n.d.

Maier, N. R. F. *Problem Solving and Creativity in Individuals and Groups.* Belmont, Calif.: Brooks/Cole, 1970.

McDermott, D. "Planning and Acting." *Cognitive Science,* 1978, *2,* 71–109.

Moore, H. "Notes on Sculpture." In B. Ghiselin (Ed.), *The Creative Process.* New York: Mentor Books, 1955.

Polanyi, M. *Personal Knowledge.* Chicago: University of Chicago Press, 1958.

Reitman, W. R. *Cognition and Thought.* New York: Wiley, 1965.

Schwartz, D. M. "A Study of Interpersonal Problem Posing." Unpublished doctoral dissertation, University of Chicago, 1974.

Smilansky, J. "Problem Posing Ability and the Nature of Problems Students See in School." Unpublished doctoral dissertation, University of Chicago, 1977.

Webster's Third New International Dictionary of the English Language, Unabridged. Springfield, Mass.: G. & C. Merriam, 1968.

Wertheimer, M. *Productive Thinking.* New York: Harper & Row, 1945.

J. W. Getzels is the R. Wendell Harrison Distinguished Service Professor in the Departments of Education and Behavioral Sciences and in the College, University of Chicago.

Since questions can affect subsequent memory of events,
how should one interrogate eyewitnesses?

Interrogating Eyewitnesses — Good Questions and Bad

Elizabeth F. Loftus

A person who witnesses an important event such as a crime, a traffic accident, or a fire is often asked to recall the details of the event. In such a situation, even the smallest details become important: Did the intruder have light or dark hair? Was the traffic signal red or green? Did the accident occur in the northbound or southbound lane? Was the stove left on or turned off? The present chapter is concerned with interrogation as a means of ascertaining the truth about important events. The overall structure of an interrogation, as well as the specific questions asked of a witness, can have dramatic and often profound effects on the accuracy of the witness's answers.

A useful interrogation will ascertain the facts about an incident, identify those guilty of crimes, and protect innocent people from false accusation and punishment. A fuller understanding of how to conduct useful interrogations will lead ultimately to a fairer resolution of specific legally important situations. However, this is not the only benefit of improved methods of interrogation. Information from eyewitnesses to crimes, for example, is important for other reasons.

In one major statistical effort ("Surveying Crime," 1976), large numbers of individuals are being questioned routinely to determine the extent to

This research was supported by grants from the National Science Foundation to Elizabeth Loftus.

R. Hogarth (Ed.). *New Directions for Methodology of Social and Behavioral Science: Question Framing and Response Consistency*, no. 11. San Francisco: Jossey-Bass, March 1982.

which they have been victims of such crimes as rape, robbery, and assault. Information on the circumstances under which these events occurred and their effects on the victims is collected. In this study, participants are asked a series of questions about events of the preceding six months: "Did someone try to rob you by using force or threat of force? Were you at any point physically attacked by an assailant using a physical object, such as a rock or a bottle?" It is hoped that knowledge of victimization will eventually help to reduce the nation's crime rate. The designers of this national survey share a common concern with those who must investigate specific crimes and other incidents—how shall the questions be asked?

Psychologists have long studied eyewitness reports in a laboratory setting. These investigations arose because of deep interest in how individuals initially perceive an event, how well they report it after some time has elapsed, and the conditions under which their reports are more or less accurate. Although the situations investigated in these experiments are a step removed from witnessing a real crime or testifying before a jury in a courtroom, the experiments nonetheless shed light on the problems of interrogation as a means of ascertaining accurate information.

Before we discuss the psychological research on interrogation, it will be useful to make a few general comments about how people process the information that they obtain from the environment. When we experience an important event, we do not simply record the event in memory in the manner of a videotape recorder; the situation is much more complex. Many recent theoretical treatments conceive of a three-stage process (see, for example, Bourne, Dominowski, and Loftus, 1979; Crowder, 1976). First, in the acquisition stage, information is encoded, laid down, or entered in the individual's memory system. Second, in the retention stage, the new information resides in the memory. During this time, new information can become available, and it can alter memory. Third, in the retrieval stage, an individual recalls stored information. This three-stage analysis is so central to the concept of human memory that it is virtually universally accepted among psychologists.

Much of the present chapter focuses on the retrieval stage. The witness to an important event is almost invariably later asked to retrieve information about that event. Retrieval can take many forms: answering questions posed by a police officer, attending a lineup and identifying an individual who was involved in the incident, testifying in court about a recollection of the details of the incident. Over the years, psychologists have conducted experiments to determine whether variations in retrieval techniques can influence the accuracy of accounts.

The present chapter will also examine activities that occur during the retention stage. As we shall see, the questions asked of witnesses to complex events not only guide the retrieval of information about those events, but they also have another important effect. Occasionally, these questions contain new information—sometimes true and sometimes false—that can become integrated into the person's memory and thereby change it. Any subsequent attempt to retrieve information about the event taps this altered memory. In this sense, the questions asked of a witness can be viewed as a source of information to which a witness is exposed, just as conversations and newspapers can expose witnesses to information.

A critical look at the psychological research on questions leads to an understanding of the good and the bad that questions can do. Ultimately, this research will be useful in developing a theory of human question answering and techniques for more efficient interrogation.

Historical Perspective

It has been known for many years that the form of a question used can affect the accuracy of the response. A serious interest in this issue is found in the work of the French psychologist Alfred Binet (1905), better known for his work on intelligence tests. Binet's investigations were reported in English by Whipple (1909) and Burtt (1931). Binet distinguished between expectative questions, which ask directly about the existence of an object or action, and implicative questions, which imply an object's presence by asking for specific information about it. The question, "Was the gun black or silver?" is implicative, since it assumes that there was a gun and probes for its color. When the object in question did not exist, Binet received 38 percent incorrect answers to expectative questions and 62 percent incorrect answers to implicative questions, which led him to conclude that the implicative question was far more misleading. As an interesting aside, Johnson (1979) notes that the double implicative question "Did you know that what you were doing was dishonest?" is the most misleading, because one cannot use a "yes" or "no" answer to avoid the implication, but must either challenge the question directly or deny the implication. In general, Binet believed that whenever a witness was questioned, the witness's memory was to some extent forced, but that different types of questions produced different degrees of forcing. It was this forcing aspect that led to the term *leading questions.*

Research on questioning techniques continued to be done in the early 1900s in laboratories throughout Europe and America. One notable piece of research from that period was by Muscio (1916). Muscio used motion pictures to present crimes to subject-witnesses. Specific questions inquiring about the objects or actions that appeared were asked about each of the films. Muscio permitted his subjects to give a "yes," "don't know," or "no" answer to each question. When the object in question did not exist, errors occurred between 8 and 19 percent of the time, depending on the format of the questions. Of major interest was the difference in response to subjective questions ("Did you see . . . ?") and objective questions ("Was there a . . . ?"). Subjects were far more accurate in their answers to the subjective question than in their answers to the objective question. This result was due partly to greater use of the "don't know" response when the subjective form was used.

Muscio's procedures are flawed by modern standards for the conduct of experimental research. A major problem is that he did not control for item difficulty by questioning each item with all question forms. Thus, some subjects were asked "Was there a cat?" while others were asked "Did you see a dog?" Such problems as these led Burtt and Gaskill (1932) to reexamine Muscio's work and to conduct some experiments of their own. Although Burtt and Gaskill found similar questioning effects, in particular greater accuracy for subjective questions than for objective questions, the magnitude of their effects was strikingly smaller than the magnitude of the effects observed by Muscio.

A second line of inquiry concerns the differences between various methods of obtaining information from witnesses. Should witnesses be asked to report freely from memory (the narrative technique), or should they be asked specific questions (the interrogatory technique)? In the early 1920s, two studies involving a staged incident before a classful of students were conducted (Cady, 1924; Marston, 1924). In Marston's experiment, a person dressed in Western costume entered with some books under his arm and delivered a message to the teacher, who read it, made notes, and handed the message back. While the intruder waited for the note to be returned, he rubbed a knife on his gloved hand. In Cody's experiment, students observed an interaction lasting approximately five minutes between their instructor and a man introduced as a government official. In both studies, memory for details was tested. The results were similar: More errors occurred when the subject-witnesses were forced to answer specific questions than when they were free to report whatever they wished. However, those who were allowed to report freely produced accounts that were far less complete.

The same results—namely, that narrative questioning techniques produced more accurate but less complete accounts than interrogatory questioning techniques—have been obtained in two more recent studies (Lipton, 1977; Marquis, Marshall, and Oskamp, 1972). In both cases, filmed episodes were shown to subjects, and memory was subsequently tested. In Lipton's study, the narrative form produced accounts that were 9 percent accurate but that included only 21 percent of the possible details of the film. With the interrogatory form, the accounts were only 56 percent accurate, but their quantity score rose to 75 percent. Taken alone, these results could leave us in a quandary about how to question a witness. If the interrogatory technique produces answers with an increased likelihood of being incorrect, shouldn't a questioner always choose the free narrative approach? Clearly not, for witnesses may freely report some aspects of the incident, such as what happened, and fail to include information on other crucial aspects, such as what the person looked like and how long the incident lasted. Put another way, in most interrogations, both accuracy and completeness are desired. Thus, early investigators realized that in many instances both forms of questioning would need to be used, so they investigated which question to use first. With some empirical research, such as that by Snee and Lush (1941), the answer emerged: The narrative report should come first, followed by the interrogatory report. The questioner who first says, "Tell me what happened" should receive a fairly accurate description of the incident, but it will contain many gaps. This can be followed by specific questions designed to fill those gaps.

Current Research

In the past ten years, researchers have taken another look at how the wording of a question can affect the answer that it receives. One example of such work is provided by Harris (1973). Harris's subjects were told that "the experiment was a study in the accuracy of guessing measurements, and that they should make as intelligent a numerical guess as possible to each question" (p. 399). Subjects were asked one of two questions; for example, "How tall was the basketball player?" or "How short was the basketball player?" Presumably, the first question presupposes nothing about the player's height, whereas the second question presupposes that the player is short. On the average, subjects guessed about 79 inches and 69 inches, respectively, to these questions. Similar results appeared with other pairs of questions. For example, the question "How long was the movie?" led to an average estimate of 130 minutes, while the question "How short was the movie?" led to an estimate of 100 minutes. While it was not Harris's central aim to do so, he demonstrates clearly that the wording of a question can affect the answer.

The phenomenon is at work in other contexts as well, such as recall of past personal experiences. In one study (Loftus, 1975), people who believed that they were participating in market research on headache products were interviewed about their headaches and about headache products. Two questions were crucial to the experiment. One asked about the products that subjects had used in the past. It was worded in two different ways: "In terms of the total number of products, how many other products have you tried? One? Two? Three?" or "In terms of the total number of products, how many other products have you tried? One? Five? Ten?" Respondents to the question in its first form claimed to have tried an average of 3.3 other products, whereas respondents to the question in its second form claimed to have tried an average of 5.2 products.

The second key question, about frequency of headaches, was asked in two different ways: "Do you get headaches frequently, and, if so, how often?" or "Do you get headaches occasionally, and, if so, how often?" Those who responded "yes" to the first question reported an average of 2.2 headaches per week, while those who responded "yes" to the second question reported only .7 headaches per week. This study indicates that one or two words can affect a person's recollection about past personal experiences. It does not tell very much about how such words affect memory; for example, whether *frequently* raises a respondent's estimate above the true level or whether *occasionally* lowers a person's estimate. In order to determine this, one would have to know something about the person's past history.

Another way of pinpointing the inaccuracies that particular wordings produce is to have subjects in a laboratory witness an event — say, on film — and then answer specially constructed questions about what they remember. Experiments along these lines have shown that, like memory of past personal experiences, memory of recently witnessed events can be affected by question wording. In one such study (Loftus and Zanni, 1975), subjects were shown a film depicting a multiple-car accident: A car made a right-hand turn into the main stream of traffic, causing oncoming cars to stop suddenly; a five-car bumper-to-bumper collision was the result. After subjects viewed the film, they completed a questionnaire containing critical questions about items that had appeared in the film and other items that had not. For half of the subjects, critical questions began with the words "Did you see a . . . ?", as in "Did you see a broken headlight?" For the others, critical questions began with the words "Did you see the . . . ?", as in "Did you see the broken headlight?" Thus, the two questions differed only by the article *the* or the article *a,* a distinction that had intrigued Alfred Binet nearly eighty years earlier. People use the definite article *the* when they assume that the object referred to exists and that it may be familiar to the listener. The investigator who asks, "Did you see the broken headlight?" essentially says, "There was a broken headlight. Did you happen to see it?" This assumption can influence the report that a witness gives. In contrast, the indefinite article *a* does not necessarily imply existence. The results showed that witnesses who were asked *the* questions were more likely to report having seen something than witnesses who were asked *a* questions, whether or not it had appeared in the film. Once again, a seemingly superficial change in wording influenced a witness's report.

In another study (Loftus and Palmer, 1974), subjects saw films of automobile accidents and then answered questions about the accidents. The wording of questions was shown to affect numerical estimates. In particular, the question "About how fast were the cars going when they smashed into each other?" consistently elicited a higher estimate of speed than questions in which *smashed into* was replaced by *collided with, bumped into, contacted,* or *hit.* Taken together, these estimates show that the wording of a question about an event can influence the answer given. The same effect has been observed when a person reports his or her own experiences, describes events recently witnessed, or answers a general question not based on any specific witnessed incident (for example, "How short was the movie?").

The power of questions can be seen not only in their effect on answers but also in their effect on answers to other questions asked some time afterward. This has been demonstrated quite forcefully in experiments in which people were presented with films of complex events and then asked questions containing misleading information. In one study (Loftus, 1975), I asked subjects who had just watched a film of an automobile accident, "How fast was the white sports car going when it passed the barn while traveling along the country road?" No barn existed. Other subjects were asked a control question, such as "How fast was the white sports car going while traveling along the country road?" All subjects were later asked whether they had seen a barn.

The results demonstrated clearly that the misleading question increased the likelihood that subjects would later report having seen a nonexistent barn. More than 17 percent of the subjects indicated that they had seen the barn when its existence was presupposed, whereas fewer than 3 percent indicated they they had seen the nonexistent object when it had not been presupposed. These results support the argument that such questions are effective because they contain information — in this case, false information — that becomes integrated into the respondent's recollection of the event and thereby supplements the memory.

In other studies (reviewed in Loftus, 1979), I have shown that new information can do more than simply supplement a recollection: It can occasionally alter or transform a recollection. In one study, subjects saw a series of color slides depicting successive stages in an accident involving an automobile and a pedestrian. The auto was a red Datsun traveling along a side street toward an intersection. For half of the subjects, there was a stop sign at this intersection. For the others, there was a yield sign. Immediately after subjects viewed the slides, they answered a series of questions. For half of the subjects, one of the last questions was "Did another car pass the red Datsun while it was stopped at the stop sign?" For other subjects, the words *stop sign* were replaced by the words *yield sign*. The assignment of each group of subjects to one of the two conditions produced a factorial design in which half of the subjects received consistent or correct information and the other half received misleading or incorrect information. All subjects then participated in a filler activity and were then given a forced-choice recognition test. Two slide projectors presented pairs of slides, and subjects had to select the slide that they had seen earlier from each pair. The critical pair consisted of a slide depicting the red Datsun coming to a stop sign and a nearly identical slide depicting the Datsun at a yield sign. Results indicated that when the intervening question contained information consistent with the first series of slides, 75 percent of the subjects responded accurately, while only 41 percent did so when the intervening question contained inconsistent information.

Another experiment shows that a nonexistent object can be introduced into memory without actual mention of that object (Loftus and Palmer, 1974). Subjects saw films of actual automobile accidents and answered questions about events in the films. Again, the question "About how fast were the cars going when they smashed into each other?" elicited higher estimates of speed than the same question asked with the verb *hit*. On a test administered one week later, subjects who had been given the verb *smashed* were more likely to answer "yes" to the question "Did you see any broken glass?" even though broken glass was not visible in the film.

Why did subject-witnesses recall details that never existed? When a subject sees a complex event, he or she first forms some representation of the event — an accident, in this case. When an experimenter later asks how fast the cars were going when they smashed into each other, a new piece of information is supplied, namely, that the cars smashed into each other. When these two pieces of information are integrated, the subject's memory represents the accident as more severe than it was in fact. Furthermore, since broken glass is commensurate with a severe accident, the subject is more likely to remember that there was broken glass.

Questions and the Alteration of Memory

Why do questions posed to a witness affect the witness's response? I have advanced the argument that questions are influential because they contain information — sometimes true, sometimes false — that becomes integrated into the person's recollection of the event and thereby changes the memory. Sometimes the postevent information supplements the previously acquired memory, as in the case of the barn; sometimes, it actually transforms the memory, as in the case of the stop and yield signs. It is convenient to combine these two outcomes and say that postevent information has been bonded to the original memory. Two centuries ago, the philosopher Immanuel Kant spoke of the human tendency to merge different experiences to form new concepts and ideas.

People vary in suggestibility, meaning the extent to which they will modify their recollections of an event in light of later information or the extent to which they will allow postevent information to become bonded to memory. When people who have witnessed a complex event are exposed to misleading suggestions about that event, some will modify their recollections a great deal, while others will change only slightly or not at all (Loftus, 1977). Furthermore, there are situational variables that lend themselves to maximal rather than to minimal modification.

Elsewhere (Loftus, in press), I have proposed that postevent information will be stored in memory where related information is already stored and that the bonding of postevent information can occur relatively automatically, unless the postevent information has been tagged as inappropriate. A reexamination of earlier experiments in light of this hypothesis led to the realization that we may have stumbled almost by accident upon a particularly efficient procedure for inducing bonding.

Recall the structure of the questions used to introduce misinformation. In one study, the question was "How fast was the white sports car going when it passed the barn while traveling along the country road?" In another study, the question was "Did another car pass the red Datsun while it was stopped at the stop sign?"

In both cases, the questions are rather complex, and the misleading information is embedded in a clause. In both cases, the question focuses the respondent on some aspect of the situation that is irrelevant to the misleading detail. The first question causes the respondent to focus on the speed of the white sports car, while the second causes the respondent to concentrate on whether another car passed the red Datsun at some point in time. Put another way, in both cases the misinformation is presupposed in a peripheral part of the question while attention is being directed to a central part of the question. Does the complex wording of these questions contribute to the bonding that we observe? One hypothesis is that these questions may be effective because they draw attention away from the critical detail and focus it elsewhere. When attention devoted to the critical detail is reduced, subjects may not scrutinize the detail when it is processed, although it may still be encoded into memory. In the absence of diversion, additional attention could be applied to the critical detail, which might make it easier for some subjects to tag the detail as something that they had not really noticed. The likelihood of its incorporation into memory would consequently be reduced. Thus, complex questions may be especially suited for inducing bonding of postevent information.

These ideas have been supported by a recent doctoral dissertation (Johnson, 1979). In this study, variations in question wording were examined with an eye toward determining the extent to which they influenced the likelihood that misinformation would later be recalled erroneously by a subject. In his fourth experiment, Johnson used questions containing two kinds of presuppositions, which he referred to as linguistic and logical presuppositions. The questions containing logical presuppositions were invariably longer and more complex than questions containing linguistic presuppositions. For example, compare these two ways of presupposing the existence of a "loans" sign: "Was the 'loans' sign knocked off the desk by a robber?" and "Was the woman who was sitting at the desk with the 'loans' sign biting her fingernails?" Compare also these two ways of presupposing the existence of luggage racks on the getaway car: "Were the luggage racks on the getaway car holding a large carton?" and "Was the station wagon that was equipped with luggage racks carrying a large carton?"

In the short and simple question in each pair, the linguistic presupposition is accomplished by the definite reference of the article *the*. In each case, the critical object is part of the focus of each question. In the complex question in each pair, the logical presupposition is introduced by a restrictive clause. In this case, the misinformation is not part of the focus of the question. In fact, the relative clause and the embedded item can be ignored and the question can still be answered.

Johnson's subjects participated in an experiment in which they viewed a series of slides depicting a bank robbery, answered a questionnaire, and took a final test on their memory of the details of the robbery. The questionnaire included some critical questions designed to contain either simple or complex presuppositions.

Johnson found that subjects were most likely to indicate erroneously that they had seen a particular detail when that detail was embedded in a complex question. Subjects said that they had seen a nonexistent object 28 percent of the time when the intervening question contained a complex presupposition, 20 percent of the time when it contained a simple presupposition, and between 16 and 18 percent of the time in the control conditions.

Another aspect of Johnson's results is tangential to the current point but still interesting. According to Johnson, direct mention of an object, whether it is logically or linguistically presupposed, implies that the object exists. Both types of implication could be called *identity implications,* because an entity implies itself. However, other, more indirect implications necessitate drawing an inference or performing a mental construction that includes the indirectly implied object.

Johnson made a distinction between logical and pragmatic implication. A logical implication is an entailment that necessarily follows from a statement. Thus, "George is taller than Marge" logically implies that Marge is shorter than George. Pragmatic implications are entailments that could follow from a statement, given our knowledge of the world, but do not necessarily do so. Thus, "The truck driver stirred his coffee" pragmatically implies that the driver used a spoon. However, this is not a necessary entailment, since the driver could have used something other than a spoon (Harris and Monaco, 1978). Johnson was interested in determining the relative efficiency of logical and pragmatic implications in leading us to draw inferences. Compare, for instance, these two ways of implying the existence of Western boots on one of the robbers: "Did the robber who was dressed in a Western outfit from head to toe kick a person lying on the floor?" and "Did the robber who was dressed in a Western outfit kick a person lying on the floor?" One question logically implies the existence of Western boots, while the other pragmatically implies it.

The proportion of erroneous "yes" responses to logically implied objects was .26, compared with .21 for pragmatically implied objects. This indicates that logically implying an object is roughly equivalent to mentioning it directly via a complex presupposition, while pragmatic implication is a somewhat weaker form of implication.

Johnson's finding that misinformation embedded in complex questions is likely to have a greater effect on memory than the same misinformation conveyed by simple questions has been replicated in other experiments (Loftus, in press). One explanation for this effect is that the complex question focuses the witness's attention on something other than the critical information. However, other explanations are possible. For example, the complex question may convey a stronger belief that the nonexistent object existed than the single question. A person who asks, "Was the woman who was sitting at the desk with the 'loans' sign biting her fingernails?" may communicate a stronger belief that the 'loans' sign actually existed than the person who asks, "Was the loans sign knocked off the desk?" Some experimental support for this explanation has in fact been found.

Toward a Theory of Human Question Answering

A question is asked and an answer is given. The process of answering a question is generally completed so quickly that we are largely unaware of the complexities of the cognitive processes involved. Comprehending and answering a question both draw on many realms of human cognition, including language comprehension, memory retrieval, and verbal generation. Thus, any theory of human questioning must necessarily entail a theory of memory organization and information processing.

Lehnert (1978) has noted the significance of the lack of progress made toward producing a theory of human question answering. Nevertheless, despite the inherent difficulties of this task, over the years a few things have been learned that ultimately will be useful in developing a theory of human question answering as well as in developing more efficient techniques for interrogation.

For example, at the retrieval stage we know that some questions can be answered directly, that is, with very little memory search, while other questions require inferential construction. Thus, different processes can be involved in these two types of retrieval (Camp, Lachman, and Lachman, 1980). We know that one common process that people follow in answering the inferential type of question involves first retrieving some context and then accessing the details (Williams, 1976). For example, a person who had to remember who was at a political rally might first recreate that setting and then provide the names of people who were in the setting. We know that aspects other than question wording influence recollection, for instance, what is being recalled (Lipton, 1977), who is asking the question (Marshall and Newcombe, 1966; Dodd and Bradshaw, 1980), voice intonation (Barath and Cannell, 1976), and question length (Laurent, 1972).

At the retention stage, we know that information does not reside passively in memory waiting to be accessed in response to a question. Rather, memory appears to undergo transformations when a witness is exposed to new information, and new information can be conveyed by questions. Careful attention to the language used in these questions can minimize damaging distortions. In the past, questions were seen only as a way of eliciting information. Now we know that questions can simultaneously provide information. Ongoing research efforts in both aspects of human questioning are beginning to provide an impressive body of empirical evidence that may allow the art of human questioning to develop into a science.

References

Barath, A., and Cannell, C. F. "Effect of Interviewer's Voice Intonation." *The Public Opinion Quarterly,* 1976, *40,* 370–373.

Binet, A. "La science du témoignage." *L'Année Psychologique,* 1905, *11,* 128–137.

Bourne, L. E., Dominowski, R. L., and Loftus, E. F. *Cognitive Processes.* Englewood Cliffs, N.J.: Prentice-Hall, 1979.

Burtt, H. E. *Legal Psychology.* New York: Prentice-Hall, 1931.

Burtt, H. E., and Gaskill, H. V. "Suggestibility and the Form of the Question." *Journal of Applied Psychology,* 1932, *16,* 358–373.

Cady, H. M. "On the Psychology of Testimony." *American Journal of Psychology,* 1924, *35,* 110–112.

Camp, C. J., Lachman, J. L., and Lachman, R. "Evidence for Direct-Access and Inferential Retrieval in Question Answering." *Journal of Verbal Learning and Verbal Behavior,* 1980, *19,* 583–596.

Crowder, R. G. *Principles of Learning and Memory.* Hillsdale, N.J.: Erlbaum, 1976.

Dodd, D. H., and Bradshaw, J. M. "Leading Questions and Memory: Pragmatic Constraints." *Journal of Verbal Learning and Verbal Behavior,* 1980, *19,* 695–704.

Harris, R. J. "Answering Questions Containing Marked and Unmarked Adjectives and Adverbs." *Journal of Experimental Psychology,* 1973, *97,* 399–401.

Harris, R. J., and Monaco, G. E. "Psychology of Pragmatic Implication: Information Processing Between the Lines." *Journal of Experimental Psychology: General,* 1978, *107,* 1–22.

Johnson, K. A. "The Leading Question: Isn't There An Effect?" Unpublished doctoral dissertation, University of Washington, 1979.

Laurent, A. "Effects of Question Length on Reporting Behavior in the Survey Interview." *Journal of the American Statistical Association,* 1972, *67,* 298–304.

Lehnert, W. G. *The Process of Question Answering.* Hillsdale, N.J.: Erlbaum, 1978.

Lipton, J. P. "On the Psychology of Eyewitness Testimony." *Journal of Applied Psychology,* 1977, *62,* 90–95.

Loftus, E. F. "Leading Questions and the Eyewitness Report." *Cognitive Psychology,* 1975, *7,* 560–572.

Loftus, E. F. "Shifting Human Color Memory." *Memory and Cognition,* 1977, *5,* 696–699.

Loftus, E. F. *Eyewitness Testimony.* Cambridge, Mass.: Harvard University Press, 1979.

Loftus, E. F. "Mentalmorphosis: Alterations in Memory Produced by the Mental Bonding of New Information to Old." *Attention and Performance IX,* in press.

Loftus, E. F., and Palmer, J. C. "Reconstruction of Automobile Destruction: An Example of the Interaction Between Language and Memory." *Journal of Verbal Learning and Verbal Behavior,* 1974, *13,* 585–589.

Loftus, E. F., and Zanni, G. "Eyewitness Testimony: The Influence of the Wording of a Question." *Bulletin of the Psychonomic Society,* 1975, *5,* 86–88.

Marquis, K. H., Marshall, J., and Oskamp, S. "Testimony Validity as a Function of Question Form, Atmosphere, and Item Difficulty." *Journal of Applied Social Psychology,* 1972, *2,* 167–186.

Marshall, J. C., and Newcombe, F. "Syntactic and Semantic Error in Paralexia." *Neuropsychologia,* 1966, *4,* 169–176.

Marston, W. W. "Studies in Testimony." *Journal of Criminal Law and Criminology,* 1924, *15,* 5–31.

Muscio, B. "The Influence of the Form of a Question." *British Journal of Psychology,* 1916, *8,* 351–389.

Snee, T. J., and Lush, D. E. "Interaction of the Narrative and Interrogatory Methods of Obtaining Testimony." *The Journal of Psychology,* 1941, *11,* 229–236.

"Surveying Crime." Report of the Panel for the Evaluation of Crime Surveys. Washington, D.C.: National Academy of Sciences, 1976.

Whipple, G. M. "The Observer as a Reporter: A Survey of the Psychology of Testimony." *Psychological Bulletin,* 1909, *6,* 153–170.

Williams, M. D. "Retrieval from Very Long-Term Memory." Unpublished doctoral dissertation, University of California, 1976.

Elizabeth F. Loftus is professor of psychology at the University of Washington, Seattle.

Accuracy of opinion surveys can be compromised by effects from the wording and the location of questions.

Question-Wording Effects in Surveys

Norman M. Bradburn

Anyone experienced in the analysis of data derived from sample surveys, whether they be from public opinion polls, attitude surveys, or surveys of behavior, knows that small and seemingly innocuous changes in question wording can produce quite large effects on answers. Furthermore, these effects are not limited to changes in question wording. People can respond differently to identically worded questions that appear in different contexts. In addition, changes in question wording can affect not only the univariate distributions of responses but also the covariation of answers between several questions. Since the potential of small changes in question wording for large effects on response distributions has been recognized for a long time (see, for example, Payne, 1951), it is surprising that there has not been more sustained research into ways in which question wording affects responses.

There are, I believe, two major reasons for the relative lack of concern about question wording. First, many opinion polls attempt to make only rather gross estimates of opinion levels. Given that there are many sources of response error in the survey process, it is believed that overly careful attention to question wording will do little to increase the validity of measurement. For example, the Gallup organization asked in 1954, "Do you think Communist China should or should not be admitted as a member of the United Nations?" A few months earlier, the National Opinion Research Center (NORC) had asked

R. Hogarth (Ed.). *New Directions for Methodology of Social and Behavioral Science: Question Framing and Response Consistency*, no. 11. San Francisco: Jossey-Bass, March 1982.

the question "Would you approve or disapprove of letting Communist China become a member of the United Nations?" The Gallup organiztion found that 7 percent of the population thought that Communist China should be admitted to the U.N, while 78 percent opposed admission and 15 percent had no opinion. Compare these data with NORC findings that 11 percent approved of allowing Communist China to become a member, while 79 percent opposed it and 10 percent had no opinion. While there were probably other differences between these two surveys in addition to those provided by question wording, the fact remains that an overwhelming proportion of the population opposed admission of Communist China to the U.N. ("The Polls," 1971). For many purposes of public opinion polling, a high degree of precision is unnecessary, and small variations in question wording are of little concern.

The second major reason for inattention to the influence of question wording is that much of the work by social psychologists on attitude measurement has been concerned with the structure of attitudes and their underlying dimensions. There has been less concern with the distribution of responses to single items than with the way in which items covary. Until recently, it was widely believed that, however much single items could be affected by changes in wording, covariation among items was relatively impervious to effects caused by wording changes.

Measurement of public opinion through the use of sample surveys has been going on for more than forty years. Researchers now have sufficient data over an extended period of time to study changes in attitudes on a wide variety of issues, such as attitudes toward social welfare policies, civil liberties, race prejudice, abortion, and gun control. These issues have occupied the public agenda for a considerable time. In addition, some issues that appear only sporadically on the public agenda, such as gasoline rationing and year-round daylight savings time, can also be studied profitably from a comparative point of view. For example, public opinion data concerning gasoline rationing from World War II can be useful in interpreting contemporary data. The fact that at the height of World War II only about two-thirds of the population thought that gasoline rationing was necessary provides some basis for evaluating the magnitude of public support for gasoline rationing during shortages caused by the oil embargo.

Unfortunately, the utility of such comparisons is lessened by the fact that question wording on the same topic can vary across research organizations and even across surveys carried out by the same organization at different times. Frustration arising from attempts to compare over time questions with similar but not identical wording has renewed interest in question wording and its potential effects on responses. In order to make comparisons, it is important to know when wording changes make a difference and when they do not.

There is still no theoretical framework that enables us to predict which types of question changes will be substantively important and which will not.

The purpose of this chapter is to summarize some instances of question-wording changes that have caused substantive differences in responses as well as to make some generalizations about factors that affect the relationships between questions and answers. It is hoped that this effort will focus attention on an important problem that needs more systematic research.

Question Wording and Question Meaning

Questioning is a form of communication between people in which a questioner tries to elicit information from a respondent. Questioners seek a particular kind of information and try to convey that desire through the questioning process. For adequate communication to take place, the respondent must understand the meaning of the question. At the same time, the questioner must understand the meaning of the response and judge whether it is a satisfactory answer to the question. Speaking the same language is a necessary but not sufficient condition for this communication process to take place.

Current survey practice relies almost entirely on standardized questions; that is, on questions worded in the same way for all respondents. The assumption is that questions can be framed in terms that are widely understood in the same way and that their meaning will be correctly understood by almost everyone. It is recognized that there are idiosyncratic meanings and that there are regional and subcultural differences in the meanings attached to individual words. Nevertheless, survey researchers believe that it is possible to construct questions that will be understood by almost all English speakers in the population. Non-English speakers are provided with language-specific translations (which pose problems of meaning of their own), or, if no translator is available, they are omitted from the sample.

Critics of survey research have long been skeptical of the use of standardized questions with heterogeneous populations. Others argue that, while it is possible to measure some types of rather superficial attitudes through standardized questions, one sacrifices richness and depth of meaning in exchange for the standardization.

Given the importance of standardization, surprisingly little research has investigated the way in which the meaning of questions is successfully communicated to respondents in the survey context. One of the few studies is that by Dohrenwend (1965). She conducted a controlled laboratory experiment that examined the standardization of questioning in interviews, the effect of the interviewers, and the experience about which the respondents were interviewed. Experimental conditions varied both the form of the questions (standardized versus varied) and the subject matter of the interview (behavior versus attitudes). Interviews were divided into two parts, so that each contained standardized and nonstandardized questions and covered both behavior and attitudes in a carefully counterbalanced design. Four highly experienced interviewers conducted two interviews in each of the four experimental conditions, yielding thirty-two interviews in all. Respondents were female undergraduates at Cornell, who were interviewed about their experiences in controlled pseudoexperiments preceding the experimental interviews. Activities of the pseudoexperiment were recorded so that behavioral aspects of what went on during the experimental period could be validated.

The results indicated that standardized questions were not inferior to nonstandardized questions, although the data were not unequivocal. Relatively little difference was produced by question forms, although there was some interaction with interviewers, which suggests that some interviewers were better with one form of question than with the other. There was also interaction with subject matter, such that, when the subject matter was behavior, but not when it was a subjective evaluation, responses to unstandardized questions contained more self-revelation than responses to standardized questions. Responses to unstandardized questions about attitudes were also significantly shorter than responses to unstandardized questions about behavior. Length of responses to standardized questions did not vary with the subject matter. Dohrenwend suggests that standardized questions exert a tighter control over respondents' answers and thus elicit better responses in cases where respondents are reluctant and restrict their answers on unstandardized questions.

The data provided no evidence that unstandardized questions are superior in obtaining responses of greater depth or validity, but there was a higher interaction involving form, subject matter, and interviewer. This effect was due to the inability of one interviewer to use unstandardized questions to elicit valid behavioral reports. This result raises the possibility that unstandardized questioning may be more susceptible to interviewer effects. Depth in response, as measured by the proportion of statements that were judged self-revealing, was not different in general between the two forms of questions, but again there was an interaction. Dohrenwend argues that this interaction contradicts the notion that standardized questions are ineffective for in-depth interviewing.

Even the most devoted practitioner of standardized questioning is aware that there are many ambiguities in questions and that extensive pretesting is necessary in order to develop good standardized questions. Unfortunately, due to budget limitations and the belief (mentioned earlier) that for many topics question wording is not of overriding importance, many studies do not pretest questions adequately.

Belson (1968) suggested a technique for the pretested phase whereby respondents are asked to repeat their understanding of the meaning of the question in their own words. This technique is analogous to back translating, when questions are translated into another language. On the basis of his use of this technique, Belson concludes pessimistically that even with well-developed, simplified questionnaires, many respondents do not understand the question as it was intended by the researcher.

Extensive pretesting may be useful even with previously used questions, particularly if the researcher is adapting questions for a sample with which the question has not been used. For example, a NORC interviewer pretesting items from a well-known attitude scale on a sample of adolescents reported one interesting interpretation of the item "It is better not to try to plan when to have children but just to accept them when they come." Asked about the meaning of that item, this respondent answered, "Of course, you accept them when they come — you can't just leave them in the hospital."

Sometimes, questions used in public opinion research are about topics that have no precise meaning, such as U.S. policy toward Israel, government fiscal policy, liberalism, conservatism, big business, or the government in Washington; as a result, they can be understood in different ways by different respondents.

Sometimes, respondents recognize that the referent of the question is ambiguous and ask for clarification. In response to the question "What things do you like best about living in this neighborhood?" a respondent might ask sensibly, "What do you mean by 'this neighborhood'?" Unless the researcher has a specific definition in mind and supplies it to respondents, respondents are usually instructed to define the concept for themselves. This, of course, is what people do implicitly with the concepts in all questions. However, the range in interpretation may be greater than the investigator understands, and this can make it difficult to interpret the responses.

Fee (1979) has investigated the meanings of some common political symbols used in public opinion studies. She adopted a variant of Belson's methods, in which people were asked to elaborate on their understanding of particular symbols, such as federal government and big business. She found that there were clusters of meanings, which gave rise to quite different interpretations of questions. For example, she found at least nine meanings for the term *energy crisis*. For the symbol *big government*, which was what she investigated most thoroughly, she found four distinct images: One defined big government in terms of welfare, socialism, and overspending; another viewed big government in terms of big business and government for the wealthy; a third defined big government in terms of a combination of federal control and diminished state's rights; and the fourth saw big government as bureaucracy and a lack of democratic process. Different kinds of people tended to hold different images, which were related to different attitudes. Without knowing which image respondents held, it would be difficult to interpret their responses to questions about big government.

In sum, use of standardized questions in surveys is based on three assumptions: that their meaning is widely shared, that respondents understand a given stimulus in roughly equivalent ways, that responses will be given in a manner that allows them to be compared by the researcher. To some extent, these assumptions can be tested by extensive pretesting in which the meaning of the questions asked is ascertained from a heterogeneous set of respondents. Since variations in question wording can affect how respondents interpret questions, work on question wording should concentrate on ways in which the wording of questions affects meaning.

Question Elements That Change Meaning

In the absence of a general theory of question meaning, I shall adopt a rather arbitrary classification of ways in which question elements can affect meaning. The discussion will be organized into three sections: internal question wording, response categories, and context (that is, the relation of questions to other questions in the questionnaire).

Internal Question Wording. Perhaps the most common way in which changes in question wording can change the meaning of questions is by focusing attention on a particular meaning of the question, which reduces its generality. An example of the effect of increasing the specificity is seen in questions from a Gallup Poll of May–June 1945:

> Do you think the government should give money to workers who are unemployed for a limited length of time until they can find another job? [yes: 63 percent; no: 32 percent; don't know: 5 percent]
>
> It has been proposed that unemployed workers with dependents be given up to $25 per week by the government for as many as twenty-six weeks during one year while they are out of work and looking for a job. Do you favor or oppose this plan? [yes: 46 percent; no: 42 percent; don't know: 12 percent]
>
> Would you be willing to pay higher taxes to give unemployed persons up to $25 a week for twenty-six weeks if they fail to find satisfactory jobs? [yes: 34 percent; no: 54 percent; don't know: 12 percent]

Support for unemployment compensation in general was quite high, but it shrank as specific amounts of money and time were added to the question, and it decreased even more when the necessity of paying higher taxes to support such a system was introduced.

Another example of the effects of situational qualification to general questions has been analyzed by Smith (1980). In the 1973 and 1975 General Social Surveys, respondents were asked first, "Are there any situations that you can imagine in which you would approve of a man punching an adult male stranger?" Respondents were then asked a series of questions about specific conditions under which they might approve of such an action, such as the stranger had hit the man's child after the child had accidently damaged the stranger's car or the stranger was beating up a woman and the man saw it. In fact, 84 percent of those who disapproved of hitting an adult stranger "in any situation [that they] could imagine" went on to indicate their approval in one or more of the five situations presented. The disapprovers averaged about two approvals for hitting when specific situations were described. Smith suggests that many respondents are not interpreting the general question as literally asked but responding instead to the absolute phrase "Are there any situations that you can imagine" as if it meant "In the situations that you can easily think of" or simply "in general."

Question wordings that appear to be logically equivalent can produce quite different responses. The most notable example of this type of effect is seen with positive-negative wording reversals. Approval of a positively worded attitudinal statement is frequently not the same as disapproval of the same attitude when it is expressed negatively. Payne (1951) offers one example, taken from Rugg (1941): "Do you think the United States should allow public speeches against democracy? Do you think the United States should forbid public speeches against democracy?" To the first question, 21 percent responded that speeches against democracy should be allowed, while 39 percent said that such speeches should not be forbidden. Similarly, 62 percent said that such speeches should not be allowed, but only 46 percent said that they should be forbidden. Other respondents had no opinion on the matter.

Similar, if not synonymous, terms that indicate a positive orientation toward an attitude object can have different connotations and yield different responses. For example, the terms *approve* and *disapprove*, *like* and *dislike* are frequently used in attitude questions, although little attention has been paid to the possible differences in implication between the two terms. An empirical test of the similarities of these terms was obtained in the context of questions about year-round daylight savings time (Murray and others, 1974). These two questions were asked of respondents in a national probability sample polled in March and April 1974:

> As you know, the United States Congress put our country back on Daylight Savings Time this winter as part of a two-year experiment to try to save energy. Some people think that we should continue to have Daylight Savings Time all year round, that is, not turn the clocks back at the end of next October. Would you approve or disapprove of remaining on Daylight Savings Time all year round next year, or don't you care one way or the other?

> As you know, we recently switched from Standard Time to Daylight Savings Time. That means that it now gets light an hour later in the morning than before we switched over. It also means that it now gets dark an hour later in the evening than before we switched over. How do you feel about being on Daylight Savings Time now? Would you say you like it very much, like it somewhat, dislike it somewhat, or dislike it very much?

A cross-tabulation of the responses indicated that, while the two items were quite highly correlated, it was still possible for people to like something without approving of it and to approve of something without liking it. Of those who liked year-round daylight savings very much, only 86 pecent approved of it, while 10 percent of those who disliked it very much also approved of it.

Response Categories. Questions in surveys sometimes include the response categories within the question, as in "Would you say that your own health, in general, is excellent, good, fair, or poor?" In other forms of survey questions, response categories are shown to respondents on cards. Alternatively, particularly when numerical answers are required, no response category is given to the respondent; the interviewer simply records the responses verbatim.

The effects of these different types of response categories are not well understood, although there is abundant evidence that the type of response category offered to respondents can affect responses in fairly marked ways. One question of considerable concern to opinion researchers is whether bipolar questions should include a middle alternative; that is, in questions that have such response categories as favor/oppose and approve/disapprove. The middle alternative would represent something like indifference. In general, the practice in survey research has been to omit middle categories to try to push respondents toward one or the other term of a bipolar choice. It is clear from empirical work that the addition of an explicit middle alternative increases the size of the category and that, in a forced-choice situation, people are expressing opinions for or against the attitude object even though the strength of their opinions may be quite low.

Recent studies by Schuman and Presser (1979) show that the inclusion of a middle alternative in forced-choice attitude questions does not affect the ratio of the positive and negative positions. Indeed, as generally believed, those who do not feel very strongly about an issue are more susceptible to the effect of the number of response categories than those who do feel strongly about the issue. Furthermore, Schuman and Presser found that, for most items studied, inclusion of the middle category did not change the relationship between the opinion item and such respondent background characteristics as education but that, in at least one instance, it did change the relationships among different opinion items.

An experiment by Bradburn, Sudman, and Associates (1979) compared the effects of precoded response categories and verbatim recording on behavioral reports of such things as alcohol consumption. One question was asked only of those who reported drinking beer during the previous year: "On the average, about how many bottles, cans or glasses of beer did you drink at one time?" In the precoded version, the codes were 1, 2, 3, 4, 5, 6 or more. In the open-ended version, there were no codes, and the interviewer simply wrote down the number given by the respondents.

Estimates of beer consumption based on open-ended questions were about 60 percent greater than estimates based on precoded responses. The reasons for this difference are not clearly understood. It is probable that the distribution of alcohol consumption has a long tail on the high side. Thus, those who report more consumption than the highest precoded category allows for tend to increase the average. It is also possible that the precodes were interpreted as a sort of implicit norm and that some high consumers were reluctant to place themselves in the highest category, particularly if they did not consider themselves heavy drinkers.

Contextual Meaning. Questions are not asked in a vacuum. Even the question that appears first in a questionnaire has been preceded by some introductory material. An identically worded question that appears several times in one questionnaire can produce quite different responses from the same person. Questions that are quite closely related, particularly questions that are related to the same attitude object, can work to increase the saliency of aspects of the opinion under inquiry For example, one early study (American Marketing Association, 1937) reported results of a study of women's attitudes about advertising. Women's attitudes were more positive when questions about advertising followed questions about dresses than they were when advertising questions preceded the dress questions. The explanation offered for this finding was that women tended to think about all types of advertising if the questions were not preceded by a more narrowly defining set of questions concerning dresses. Since the women's attitudes about dress advertising were more favorable than their attitudes about other types of advertising, they gave more favorable responses to questions that followed questions about dress advertising.

A somewhat similar finding was reported by Noelle-Neumann (1970), who examined the designation of various foods as particularly "German." This study was part of an exploration of the image of three basic foodstuffs. In one form of the questionnaire, respondents were asked first about potatoes, then about rice; in another form of the same questionnaire, this order was reversed. When respondents were asked about potatoes first, 30 percent said that potatoes were particularly "German." However, when respondents were asked about rice first, 48 percent said that potatoes were particularly "German." A similar order effect was found for the pair noodles-rice.

More recently, it has been observed that when a general question and a related, more specific question are asked together, the general question can be affected by its position, while the more specific question is not. Take, for example, two questions that appeared in the 1980 General Social Survey: "Taking things all together, how would you describe your marriage? Would you say that your marriage is very happy, pretty happy, or not too happy?" and "Taken all together, how would you say things are these days—would you say that you are very happy, pretty happy, or not too happy?" The results of a split-ballot experiment, in which the order of these questions was rotated, indicated that responses to the general question about overall happiness were affected by the order in which the questions were asked, while the question on marriage happiness was not affected by the order.

One theory which accounts for these findings is that when the general question comes first, it is answered in terms of one's whole life, including marriage. When the specific question on marriage happiness comes first, the overall happiness question is interpreted as referring to all other aspects of life. It is as if respondents who have been asked a question about marriage happiness exclude this part of their lives from further consideration.

Similar findings have been reported by Schuman and Presser (1981) for general and specific attitude items relating to abortion. The effect may reflect attempts to avoid giving redundant responses. That is, having answered the detailed question first, respondents may feel that they are repeating themselves if they take into consideration the answer to the more specific question. When respondents answer the general question first, it is clear that subsequent, specific questions are subsets of the general ones. Answers to the specific questions may well be different from answers to the general ones. Thus, it does not seem to be redundant to answer such questions.

Another situation in which order effects may appear arises with questions that have close substantive relationship one to another, such that the answers to one question have logical implications to the answers for the others. A considerable amount of attitude research suggests that there is a general strain toward consistency in attitudes. The order in which questions are asked may increase or decrease the cues for such consistency. A well-known study by Cantril and Research Associates (1944) shows that questions about the willingness of respondents to allow Americans to enlist in the British and German armies before 1941 was affected by the order in which the questions were asked. More respondents were willing to allow Americans to enlist in the German army when this question followed a similar question about their enlisting in the British army than they did when the questions were asked in reverse order. Similiar order effects were reported by Hyman and Sheatsley (1950) in a survey regarding reciprocity between the U.S.S.R. and the United States in the free exchange of news. These situations involved questions of differing degrees of popularity, but both involved the same underlying value. When the more popular item comes first, it appears to have the effect of heightening the value, so that it applies to the second and less powerful instance. However, when the less popular instance comes first, it does not appear to reduce support for the more popular item.

One of the better-studied sets of questions is the series on confidence in major national institutions (Ladd, 1976–1977; Smith, 1979; Turner and Krauss, 1978). A split-ballot experiment to test a context hypothesis was conducted in the 1978 General Social Survey (GSS). It had been observed that a Harris survey done at about the same time as the 1976 GSS showed a considerably more negative appraisal of the institutional leadership of the United States than indicated by the GSS. In the GSS, the confidence item was the first question; in the Harris, the confidence questions came shortly after a six-point alienation index consisting of six negative statements about elite and leadership groups and about efficacy and political participation. In the split-ballot experiment, a randomly preselected half of the sample was asked the alienation questions immediately before the confidence question; the other half of the sample was asked the confidence question immediately before the alienation questions. Differences between the two forms were not large, but they did tend to favor the context hypothesis. Questions were asked about confidence in thirteen institutions. Only confidence in major companies showed a statistically significant difference between the two forms of the questionnaire.

In sum, while it is clear that some questions are affected by their relation to other questions, many questions are relatively impervious to the context in which they appear. We are still a long way from understanding why contextual effects occur where they do.

Conclusions

It is clear that small wording changes can have large effects on responses, that the same question can take on different meanings when asked in different contexts, and that even the same questions asked in the same context can be interpreted in different ways by different respondents. It is also true that some wording changes do not make much difference to respondents and that some questions are relatively impervious to context. Faced with ignorance about the conditions under which wording and context make a substantial difference, some researchers abandon standardized questions altogether. Others take the position that there are many sources of error in data and that response effects due to question wording are just another source of random error that contributes to noise in the data. Both reactions are understandable, although neither is adequate to the problem. Only when we have a thorough understanding of the ways in which question variations affect responses will we be able to improve the quality of our data. Some of the research described in this paper goes part of the way toward increasing our understanding, but much more systematic research, conducted within a conceptual framework that permits cumulative knowledge, will be necessary before we can make significant progress toward this goal.

References

American Marketing Association. *The Technique of Marketing Research.* New York: Mc-Graw-Hill, 1937.

Belson, W. A. "Respondent Understanding of Survey Questions." *Polls*, 1968, *3* (1), 1–13.

Bradburn, N. M., Sudman, S., and Associates. *Improving Interview Method and Questionnaire Design: Response Effects to Threatening Questions in Survey Research.* San Francisco: Jossey-Bass, 1979.

Cantril, H., and Research Associates. *Gauging Public Opinion.* Princeton, N.J.: Princeton University Press, 1944.

Dohrenwend, B. A. "Some Effects of Open and Closed Questions on Respondents' Answers." *Human Organization*, 1965, *24*, 175–184.

Fee, J. "Symbols and Attitudes: How People Think About Politics." Unpublished doctoral dissertation, University of Chicago, 1979.

Hyman, H. H., and Sheatsley, P. B. "The Current Status of American Public Opinion." In J. C. Payne (Ed.), *In the Teaching of Contemporary Affairs: Twenty-First Yearbook of the National Council for the Social Studies.* Washington, D.C.: National Council for the Social Studies, 1950.

Ladd, E. C., Jr. "The Polls: The Question of Confidence." *Public Opinion Quarterly,* 1976–1977, *40,* 544–556.

Murray, J., and others. "The Impact of the 1973–1974 Oil Embargo on the American Household." Report No. 126. Chicago: National Opinion Research Center, 1974.

Noelle-Neumann, E. "Wanted: Rules for Wording Structured Questionnaires." *Public Opinion Quarterly,* 1970, *34,* 191–201.

Payne, S. L. *The Art of Asking Questions.* Princeton, N. J.: Princeton University Press, 1951.

"The Polls." *Public Opinion Quarterly,* 1971, *35,* 125–126.

Rugg, D. "Experiment in Wording Questions, II." *Public Opinion Quarterly,* 1941, *5* (1) 91–92.

Schuman, H., and Presser, S. "The Assessment of 'No Opinion' in Attitude Surveys." In K. F. Schuessler (Ed.), *Sociological Methodology 1980.* San Francisco: Jossey-Bass, 1979.

Schuman, H., and Presser, S. *Questions and Answers in Attitude Surveys: Experiments on Question Form, Wording, and Context.* New York: Academic Press, 1981.

Smith, T. "Can We Have Confidence in Confidence? Revisited." Technical Report No. 11. Chicago: National Opinion Research Center, 1979.

Smith, T. "Situational Qualifications to Generalized Absolutes: An Analysis of 'Appraisal of Hitting' Questions and the General Social Surveys." Technical Report No. 21. Chicago: National Opinion Research Center, 1980.

Turner, C., and Krauss, E. "Fallible Indicators of the Subjective State of the Nation." *American Psychologist,* 1978, *33,* 456–470.

Norman M. Bradburn is the Tiffany and Margaret Blake Distinguished Service Professor in behavioral sciences at the Graduate School of Business and the College, University of Chicago and director of the National Opinion Research Center (NORC).

Answering questions and understanding what you read
or hear depends on the context.

The Importance of Context in
Understanding Discourse

Tom Trabasso

Suppose you hear this sentence (1): Mary had a little lamb. What do you think about? A nursery rhyme? Mother Goose? A little girl in a shepherd's dress with a crook? A fleecy, frolicking farm animal? A scene in a farmyard?

Now read this sentence (2) in conjunction with (1): Its fleece was white as snow. The pair of sentences, (1) and (2), confirms one interpretation of (1) — that Mary is a character from a well-known nursery rhyme, a little girl who is followed about by her pet lamb. In this interpretation, the verb *had* refers to ownership, and the possessive pronoun *its* refers to the lamb. Thus, you interpret that Mary owns the lamb, which owns a fleece of wool.

Note, however, that sentences (1) and (2) do not explicitly tell you that Mary was a little girl, that the lamb is a living animal, that the lamb is the little girl's pet, that the lamb has a wool fleece, or that the lamb follows Mary. While the process of making these interpretations may appear to be automatic, automatic to the point of self-evidence, sentence (1) lends itself to other interpretations.

For example, consider sentence (1) in the context of sentence (3): She spilled gravy and mint jelly on her dress. In this pairing, the lamb does not

The writing of this chapter was supported by National Institute of Education grant NIE-G-79-0125 to Tom Trabasso.

R. Hogarth (Ed.). *New Directions for Methodology of Social and Behavioral Science: Question Framing and Response Consistency*, no. 11. San Francisco: Jossey-Bass, March 1982.

78

fare so well. The references to gravy and mint jelly indicate that the lamb is more probably a meal than a pet. One does not infer anything about a wool fleece or its color. However, Mary is still human and female, since the pronouns *she* and *her* and the noun *dress* allow this inference. Mary may also still be a child, since children are more likely than adults to spill food on themselves. Certainly Mary is no longer the character in the nursery rhyme.

Now, pair sentence (4) with sentence (1) and note how the interpretation shifts: The delivery was a difficult one, and afterwards the vet needed a drink. Here (1) and (4) lead to the interpretation that Mary had given birth to a lamb and that she is a mature, female sheep, not a little girl. This arises from the references to the veterinarian and to a difficult delivery. *The vet* is a contraction of the name of an individual, probably an adult, whose profession is to tend to animals that are sick or in need of medical assistance. The *drink* is likely to be alcoholic; presumably, it is taken to enable the vet to relax after the difficult delivery of the newborn lamb.

In these three pairs of sentences, we can see how comprehension of discourse or of a string of utterances depends upon the sentences and the knowledge that they activate in a reader or a listener. A given sentence lends itself to many levels of interpretation, and the level that is chosen depends upon context. In these three examples the second sentence serves as a context for interpreting the first. This context leads to radically different interpretations of the same objective event, namely sentence (1).

A second message here is that the reader's understanding of sentence (1) depended, in each pair, upon a vast range of assumptions and knowledge. The reader needs to know about nursery rhymes, ownership, pets, little girls, sheep, food, animal births and caretakers, and alcohol. Each of these concepts contributed, in part and interactively across the two sentence contexts, to the reader's construction of a coherent interpretation of the sentence pairs. The meaning of sentence (1) is inherently ambiguous. Sentences (2), (3), and (4) invoke knowledge and provide three radically different contexts which allow meanings implicit in the message to be inferred. The knowledge activated by sentences (2), (3), and (4) appears to be necessary in order to interpret sentence (1) in the three ways just described (Trabasso, 1981).

The idea that the ability to understand and remember is a joint function of relationships between sentences and activated knowledge is hardly new. It was a central part of Buhler's (1908) field theory. In this view, comprehension occurs when the listener and the speaker share a common semantic field in the act of communication.

Activating Context Prior to Understanding

The field could also be a set of conditions or circumstances in which events occur. Absence of this set could cause severe difficulties in comprehension. A good example of a contextual field and its effects on the understanding of a passage comes from Bransford and Johnson (1972). Read the following passage: "The procedure is actually quite simple. First you arrange items into different groups. Of course, one pile may be sufficient depending upon how much there is to do. If you have to go somewhere else due to the lack of facilities, that is the next step; otherwise, you are pretty well set. It is important not to overdo things. That is, it is better to do too few things at once than too many. In the short run this may not seem important but complications can easily arise. A mistake can be expensive as well. At first, the whole procedure will seem complicated. Soon, however, it will become just another facet of life. It is difficult to foresee any end to the necessity for this task in the immediate future, but then, one never can tell. After the procedure is completed, one arranges the materials into different groups again. Then they can be put into their appropriate places. Eventually they will be used once more and the whole cycle will then have to be repeated. However, that is part of life" (Bransford and Johnson, 1972, p. 400).

How well did you understand this passage? If your understanding was represented on a seven-point scale, with one being "not at all" and seven "understood very well," what would your rating be? How well were you able to remember the passage? If the passage and your recalled sentences were scored into idea units (roughly, propositions involving one predicate), how many of eighteen units would you recall? If you are like Bransford and Johnson's college students, you would give the passage a two or "not very comprehensible" rating, and you would probably remember three or four units. In the absence of any context, Bransford and Johnson's subjects rated the passage 2.29 on average and recalled 2.82 units, about 16 percent.

If you haven't already guessed, the context is "washing clothes." Now, reread the passage with this topic in mind. You will verify that the passage makes more sense. In the Bransford and Johnson study, both comprehension and recall increased when people were told the topic before they read the passage. Their average rating on the seven-point scale was 4.5, which lies between "somewhat comprehensible" and "comprehensible." The average number of idea units recalled was 5.83, or 32 percent, twice as many as the units recalled by those who had no knowledge of the topic. Thus, activating the appropriate field prior to reading enhanced interpretation of the discourse and memory for it.

Models for Comprehending

How does the presence of the contextual field help comprehension and recall? Knowing the topic is washing clothes activates a model of stored information. This model can be used to generate and test expectations about the incoming information or to verify through instantiation each successive proposition that is stated in relatively abstract, general terms (Anderson and McGaw, 1973).

When we do not have a context prior to reading, the first sentences of the text serve as our data structure in inferring one. Once a context or a model is inferred, we test incoming sentence meanings against it. If a sentence fits the model, it is retained; if it leads to mismatches or falsification of events consistent with the model, we abandon the model and infer a new one.

This process of model construction and verification can be illustrated by use of three sentences from Collins, Brown, and Larkin (1981). Examine your thought processes as you progress through three events: (5) He plunked down $5 at the window. (6) She tried to give him $2.50, but he refused to take it. (7) So when they got inside, she bought him a large bag of popcorn.

Collins, Brown, and Larkin found that most of their subjects interpreted event (5) as occurring at a race track and a betting window. The amount of money and the action of "plunking down" seem to support this contextual field interpretation. However, upon hearing event (6), listeners became confused and questioned their original interpretation. The amount of $2.50 violates betting expectations, since the most usual amount of bet is $2 or $5. Further, his act of refusal is uninterpretable in the assumed context. Listeners now try to construct a new model, but event (6) does not provide sufficient data. Event (7) clarifies the situation. It allows an inference that the couple are at the movies. Add to this the further assumption that they are going dutch on a date, and all the events of (5), (6), and (7) become comprehensible, that is, consistent with the model. (5) can be verified by his buying tickets; (6) by his date's trying to pay him for her share and his refusing; and (7) by her treating him by buying the popcorn.

In this example, one can see clearly how the particular, concrete events in (5), (6), and (7) are used to instantiate a general model. In the example of washing clothes from Bransford and Johnson, the specific, concrete events are stored as a network structure under the topic, and each general statement in the passage can be interpreted against them. If you have washed clothes, it is easy to understand that you separate white from colored garments, that washing machines have limited capacities and should not be overloaded, that clothes will become dirty once more and that the process is repetitive, that clothes need to be resorted into types and put away in dressers or closets when the washing is done, and so forth. The notion that instantiation is necessary to interpretation is supported by a study by Raye cited in Bransford (1979). Raye substituted eleven concrete nouns in the washing clothes passage and found both that recall substantially increased and that comprehensibility ratings were as high as they were when people were aware of the topic before they read the passage.

Besides serving to instantiate or verify each proposition as it occurs, the instantiated events are assimilated into an organized system already in memory. These systems, variously called *schemata* (Bartlett, 1932), *frames* (Minsky, 1975), *grammars* (Mandler and Johnson, 1977; Rumelhart, 1975; Stein and Glenn, 1979), *scripts* (Schank and Abelson, 1977), and *causal chains* (Schank,

1975; Warren, Nicholas, and Trabasso, 1979) allow for the rapid construction of an organized, coherent structure to be used in storage and retrieval of the events in a text of connected discourse. Since the schemata or models may already be organized, their use reduces processing demands and provides efficient storage and retrieval. I shall discuss these structures further. I have just tried to suggest how these models are used both for comprehension and recall and thereby accounted for the findings of Bransford and Johnson.

The Bransford and Johnson findings suggest that the contextual field evoked prior to the initial reading or hearing of the connected discourse facilitates comprehension and encoding. Bransford and Johnson tested this implication by examining the effect of presenting a context after the students read the clothes washing passage. Becoming aware of the topic after the fact had no apparent benefit. Neither the comprehension ratings (average 2.12) nor the recall ratings (average 2.65, or 14.7 percent) differed appreciably from the no-topic control group's performance, just described.

The passage used by Bransford and Johnson is extremely resistant to interpretation by reading. If more meaningful, less abstract material is used, it becomes possible to show that topics or models can operate both at encoding and later in retrieval. That is, when material is comprehensible in terms of one model, other aspects of the discourse may be recollected via an alternative model.

Schemata Effects at Encoding and in Retrieval

In order to study the effect when different points of view of a text are taken during encoding or comprehension and during retrieval, Pichert and Anderson (1977) asked two groups of college students to read a passage from one point of view. Then, students recalled the passage. Following this, they were given a different point of view and asked to recall the passage a second time. The passage described two boys playing in a house. In the story, the boys moved about the house, and the location and content of the various rooms that they entered and in which they played was described. First, one group read the passage from the perspective of a prospective homebuyer; the other group read it from the perspective of a burglar. In the first recall, each group recalled more details that were appropriate to each perspective. The home buyers recalled more detail about room layout and condition of plumbing, whereas the burglars remembered more detail about expensive items, such as jewelry or television sets. These data are consistent with the idea that the perspective is used as a model for interpreting the passages and for encoding details that are consistent with the model. When the perspectives were shifted, however, students were able to recall items relevant to the new perspective that they had not recalled the first time. These data indicate that a context acquired subsequent to hearing a text can guide comprehension and selection of information for retrieval or reporting. Thus, not only is context necessary for interpretation but it can also be used during recall.

One implication of these findings is reflected in a model for discourse representation and retrieval developed by Kintsch and van Dijk (1978). In their model, a text can be represented at two levels. First, the text is interpreted by microstructure rules, which process each proposition into its meanings and form a coherent representation of the text on the basis of repeated arguments or co-reference. Then, either at encoding or during retrieval, the representation in memory (microstructure) can be operated upon by macrostructures in order to create in memory or to retrieve a research report, story, or summary. In the light of the preceding discussion, it appears that the propositions of the text have to be interpreted or instantiated against other knowledge in order to create any representation. When these propositions refer directly to known events—that is, when the references are concrete—models are easy to infer; however, a representation of the text can be constructed that is capable of reinterpretation by other models or schemata.

Schemata and Comprehension

To illustrate, in concrete terms, the nature of schema as a general, organized, and abstract knowledge structure that can be used to interpret data, let us consider the concept *face*. When this concept is presented, it activates general knowledge about body parts that are highly organized; namely, an oval-shaped object with eyes, nose, mouth, and other optional features such as ears, hair, and eyebrows. These parts can each be viewed as a subschema; for example, the eye contains lids, lashes, a pupil, and so forth. In we descend through the hierarchy of subschemata, we retrieve more and more detail (Rumelhart and Ortony, 1977). When we assume that a schema is used to guide interpretation, we assume that different levels of the hierarchy are activated and that information in the input is selected for analysis and assimilation into the schema. Thus, a face can be identified first by detection of eyes, nose, and mouth in certain spatial arrangements. The details of each part can also be encoded, using the features specified in the relevant subschema. The subschemata at each level of detail serve as slots or nodes for encoding information into the representation in memory. Later, when the individual is asked to list parts that were present, the representation that was constructed is retrieved, and the elements contained in the slots or nodes are read off.

The existence of such schemata for visual objects appears to come early, and it allows for the preservation of spatial information in linguistic codes. The finding of Johnson, Perlmutter, and Trabasso (1979) confirms this: Four-year-old children, in the absence of external referents, recalled body part terms in a top-to-bottom manner. There was a high degree of association between parts within the head, the torso, and the leg sections, as if children were scanning an internal image of a schematic representation of the human figure. Similar structural associative recall was found in college students.

Story Structures as Schemata

In his analysis of recall of stories by adults, Bartlett (1932) used the term *schemata* to refer to the use of organized past experience in interpreting new information. He demonstrated the concept in well-known studies on the "War of the Ghosts" story, where the events portrayed were elaborated, distorted, or omitted in systematic fashion in recall by persons unfamiliar with the culture and origins of the tale. Recently, computer scientists studying how knowledge systems can be used to learn and understand connected discourse have relied heavily on the schemata concept.

Story schemata can be conceived in at least two ways: first, by a set of "rewrite rules" that decompose a story into components, as in the so-called "story grammars" (Mandler and Johnson, 1977; Stein and Glenn, 1979; Rumelhart, 1975, 1977; and Thorndyke, 1977); second, by hierarchical knowledge structures about characters' states, goals, actions, and outcomes (Black and Bower, 1980; Rumelhart, 1977; Stein, 1979; Stein and Trabasso, in press; Wilensky, 1978).

The rewrite rules allow a story to be broken down into its plot structure, and it is assumed that knowledge about this structure guides the comprehender's expectations about events that should occur in the story. In the Stein and Glenn (1979) grammar, the story decomposes into a setting-plus-episode structure. An episode is composed of a setting, which provides information on the characters' locale, time, and so forth; an initiating event, which causes the character to undergo various internal reactions and state changes; an internal response category, which consists of goals, cognitions or plans, and emotional reactions by the character; attempts, that is, goal-directed actions by the central character or protagonist; direct outcomes or consequences of these attempts, that is, whether the goal is achieved or not; and subsequent consequences or reactions on the part of the protagonist toward the outcome.

Given this descriptive structure, it is possible to analyze or encode stories that are heard or read at this level of abstraction and to use the resulting schema to generate another story; this is analogous to filling in the details of a face schema. Once a story is encoded, it also becomes possible to answer who, what, when, where, and why questions about it. The who, when, and where questions are usually answered with content from the setting category. The what question is usually answered with content from the initiating event, attempt, and consequence categories. The why questions are answered by goals as reasons for actions and by initiating events as reasons for goals or other natural events (Graesser, 1981; Nicholas and Trabasso, 1980).

The main reason one can answer why questions is that the categories of events in the story schema are related by causal relations. These relations are summarized by the rewrite rules of the story grammars. In one sense, the story activates a "causal field" (Mackie, 1980) through the setting statements (see the chapter by Hogarth in this volume). Here, circumstances (the normal conditions in space and time) are established for the reader and listener, and the reader or listener can readily infer the relevant factors or salient changes that allow causal inferences from them. The initiating event is a change in the causal field that produces internal state changes in the protagonist. The goals are inferred or explicitly stated desires in the protagonist to change the state of affairs by either obtaining something or removing it. These motivate or cause actions that either achieve the desired change of state (a return to normal circumstances) or do not.

The emotional reactions of the protagonist (and of others) depend directly on these outcomes as they relate to the goals. One can construct an emotional reaction sequence over the course of the story, beginning with the initiating event, that is consistent with some psychoanalytic classifications of emotions (Dahl and Stengel, 1978). In Dahl and Stengel's system, an emotion is broken down into its component emotional reactions toward objects, encompassing the precipitating events (initiating events), wishes (goals), and consummatory acts (attempts). How the character feels about himself depends on how well the acts are helping to achieve the goals or whether the goals are achieved.

To illustrate, John sees Mary, an attractive classmate, at a party (initiating event). John feels attracted to Mary (internal response, emotion: loving). John thinks about engaging Mary in conversation (goal: to possess Mary). John starts to walk over to Mary through a crowd of people, and Mary looks at John (attempt, message: things are going well; emotion: excitement). Mary suddenly turns to Fred, a friend of John's (consequence, message: things are not going well; emotion: anxiety). Fred joins hands with Mary, and they leave the room. John feels depressed (reaction, message: goal failure; possible feeling toward Fred and Mary: anger).

Schematic notions of episodic structures in stories thus can be used to answer questions about internal, affective states. Moreover, these affective states are directed toward others or felt about oneself. This distinction points to a double ambiguity when we ask, "How does John feel?" The first ambiguity is how the person feels toward other persons, and the second ambiguity is how the person feels about what is occurring to him as it relates to his goals. Thus, questions about affect need to be qualified in terms of the source or by how well things are going in relation to the person's goals.

This kind of schematic knowledge appears early in development. Children as young as three years of age make semantic distinctions between causes and consequences of positive and negative emotional states and between self and other emotions (Surbey, 1979; Trabasso, Stein, and Johnson, in press).

In the goal-directed approaches to story comprehension, the representation of the story is structured by an importance hierarchy of goal-action-outcome sequences (Black and Bower, 1980; Rumelhart, 1977; Wilensky, 1978). Higher levels in the hierarchy correspond to major goals, and lower levels correspond to subgoals and other detail. The why questions here may have to be more specific in order to help a person to understand. For example, in a story used by Stein, Trabasso, and Garfin (1979), first-, third-, and seventh-grade children were asked why a character in a story stole a cat's whisker. Younger children focused on the subgoal, namely, to make medicine from the whisker; older children focused on the superordinate goal, to save the husband's life from a rare disease. When younger children were asked, "Why did she *want* to steal the whisker?" they, too, gave the superordinate goal of saving the husband's life. Thus, younger children were as capable of inferring internal states as the older children were. However, their answers were on goals more proximal causally to the actions in the question. Questions about goals for goals and actions elicited the desired superordinate goal.

Story schemata serve a major role in guiding comprehension or in constructing a coherent interpretation of narrative events, whether these events are fictional or part of one's own life (Hunt and Hunt, 1977). Use of these schemata in reading and listening to stories and in retelling or generating stories has been amply demonstrated. When the story that one hears "fits" the schema, that is, when it is "well formed" or complete, recall and comprehension are both high (Mandler and Johnson, 1977; Stein and Glenn, 1979). When the story parts are disordered or missing, recall and comprehension are low and the number of inferences increases (Stein and Nezworski, 1978; Wimmer, 1980). When the events are disordered, children and college students impose order according to the well-ordered form of the story described by the grammars (Mandler, 1978; Stein and Nezworski, 1978).

Words and Thought

In the preceding section, discussion centered on highly organized schemata such as stories or scripts (for example, washing clothes) that refer to episodic events in everyday life. In this section, the influence of single words on interpretation of contexts and hence on answers to questions is discussed.

One assumption of this author is that our memories are not verbatim copies of events that we experience. Rather, we reconstruct what occurred, and our reconstructions lead us to think that we are remembering accurately when in fact we are not. These errors in reconstruction can become the basis of domestic quarrels between husband and wife, and they can even influence testimony in the courtroom. Descriptions provided by leading questions or subtle wording can change expectations and interpretations.

Loftus and Palmer (1974) asked college students to watch a television film of an accident involving two cars. Then, the students were asked how fast one of the cars was going when the accident occurred. Three different verbs implying different assumed speeds were used: *bumped, collided,* and *smashed.* The students' subsequent estimates of speed varied directly with the verb used. Further, those who were asked the question with *smashed* as the verb also answered "yes" to the question "Did you see any broken glass?" The film showed no broken glass whatsoever. (See the chapter by Loftus in this volume.)

Another demonstration of how reconstruction can be influenced by single-word descriptions is found in a study by Snyder and Uranowitz (1978). Here, college students read a three-page narrative about the life of a woman. After they finished reading the story, they were given additional information about the woman's life-style. The information was that she was either lesbian or heterosexual. A control group was not given this information. The information was given either immediately or after one week's delay. All the subjects were given a recognition test one week after they read the story. The recognition test contained multiple-choice items such as (1) she occasionally dated men, (2) she never went out with men, (3) she had a steady boyfriend, (4) no information provided. The narrative said that she occasionally went out with men. Subjects who received the information that she was lesbian chose alternative (2) most frequently. Hence, people use stereotyped knowledge to reconstruct what they think was the case, which does not always correspond to what was in fact the case.

One possibility operating in both studies just cited is that the subjects viewing or reading the events either forgot what actually happened or did not encode it into memory at the time of input. If so, then their only source for reconstruction is the implied meanings of the terms used to label the events. What is also apparent is the failure of the subjects to recognize the source of their reconstruction. The label or verb becomes a part of their prior experience and indistinguishable from it. Such subtle effects of suggestion are probably more pervasive than we think!

In some instances, how one labels an event can facilitate problem solving and question answering. This is an old language and thought issue. The point is that one's interpretation of the implicit meanings of a word (which is what thinking is) guides further thinking about the topic or problem at hand. One example of such guidance is found in a study on children by Markman (1973; see also Markman and Seibert, 1976). If one shows five-year-old children three doll children and two doll adults and asks, "Are there more children or more people?" most subjects will answer "More children." The reason seems to be that subjects label the doll children *children,* interpret *or* exclusively, and label the doll adults *people* (Trabasso, Isen, Dolecki, McLanahan, Riley, and Tucker, 1978). When Markman (1973) substituted *family* for *people,* most children selected "family" as the answer. Markman's argument is that *people* is a class name, whereas *family* is a collection. Collections refer to the whole set and do not apply to the members as labels; that is, you cannot call the children *family.* Classes, however, label both the whole set and parts; that is, you can label the children, the adults, or both as *people.* Classes, thus, are more ambiguous than labels; collections are less ambiguous. In this case, the whole and not the parts is the desired answer to the question. Thus, part-whole comparisons and relations can be affected by single-word concepts in identical physical contexts.

Summary

The purpose of this chapter was to illustrate how our comprehension of events is influenced by context and the knowledge activated by it. In our comprehension of connected discourse, including the answering of questions, the interpretation of single sentences can be altered radically by prior or subsequent sentences. These different interpretations are brought about by inferential and instantiation processes. We construct a model or field for interpreting subsequent events and verify whether or not subsequent events fit the model or belong to the field. The abduction-instantiation process describes the act of comprehension.

The activation of knowledge that allows construction of an appropriate model for interpretation appears to be most critical prior to experiencing the events if the events themselves do not permit abduction (the clothes washing example). However, if interpretation and instantiation are possible, then the effects of context and activating knowledge structures also occur after encoding and prior to retrieval.

The knowledge that is activated by physical, social, sentence, or word contexts can be highly organized into structures known as schemata. These schemata, such as the setting-plus-episode structure of simple stories, can operate to help guide encoding, storage, retrieval, and generation of information about events, especially in narratives, and they can include internal states, such as goals and emotional reactions. These knowledge structures permit inferential questions of a causal nature to be answered as well as questions of other forms.

Our memories for events appear to be reconstructive. Where information is not available, we are open to subtle, implied word-meaning effects, and we construct interpretations accordingly. These reconstructions may have profound personal or social effects of a helpful or harmful variety, depending upon circumstance. Our awareness of the constructive nature of individual memory should help us to understand misunderstandings and perhaps to prevent their occurrence.

References

Anderson, R. C., and McGaw, B. "On the Representation of the Meanings of General Terms." *Journal of Experimental Psychology,* 1973, *101,* 301–306.

Bartlett, F. C. *Remembering: A Study in Experimental and Social Psychology.* Cambridge: Cambridge University Press, 1932.

Black, J. B., and Bower, G. H. "Story Understanding and Problem Solving." *Poetics,* 1980, *9,* 223–250.

Bransford, J. D. *Human Cognition.* Belmont, Calif.: Wadsworth, 1979.

Bransford, J. D., and Johnson, M. "Contextual Prerequisites for Understanding: Some Investigations of Comprehension and Recall." *Journal of Verbal Learning and Verbal Behavior,* 1972, *11,* 717–726.

Buhler, K. "Tatsachen und Probleme zu einer Psychologie der Denkvorgaenge. III. Ueber Gendankenerinnerungen." *Archives für der Gestalt Psychologie,* 1908, 1–92.

Collins, A., Brown, J. S., and Larkin, K. "Inference in Text Understanding." In R. J. Spiro, B. C. Bruce, and W. F. Brewer (Eds.), *Theoretical Issues in Reading Comprehension.* Hillsdale, N.J.: Erlbaum, 1981.

Dahl, A. D., and Stengel, B. "A Classification and Partial Test of de Rivera's Decision Theory of Emotion." *Psychoanalysis and Contemporary Thought,* 1978, *1,* 269–312.

Graesser, A. C. *Prose Comprehension Beyond the Word.* New York: Springer-Verlag, 1981.

Hunt, M., and Hunt, B. *The Divorce Experience.* Bergenfield, N.J.: New American Library, 1977.

Johnson, L. R., Perlmutter, M., and Trabasso, T. "The Leg Bone Is Connected to the Knee Bone: Children's Representation of Body Parts in Memory, Drawing, and Language." *Child Development,* 1979, *50,* 1192–1202.

Kintsch, W., and van Dijk, T. A. "Toward a Model of Text Comprehension and Production." *Psychological Review,* 1978, *85,* 363–394.

Loftus, E. F., and Palmer, J. C. "Reconstruction of Automobile Destruction: An Example of the Interaction Between Language and Memory." *Journal of Verbal Learning and Verbal Behavior,* 1974, *13,* 585–589.

Mackie, J. L. *The Cement of the Universe: A Study of Causation.* Oxford, England: Clarendon Press, 1980.

Mandler, J. M. "A Code in the Node: The Use of a Story Schema in Retrieval." *Discourse Processes,* 1978, *1,* 14–35.

Mandler, J. M., and Johnson, N. S. "Remembrance of Things Parsed: Story Structure and Recall." *Cognitive Psychology,* 1977, *9,* 111–151.

Markman, E. "The Facilitation of Part-Whole Comparisons by Use of the Collective Noun *Family.*" *Child Development,* 1973, *44,* 837–840.

Markman, E., and Seibert, J. "Classes and Collections: Internal Organization and Resulting Holistic Properties." *Cognitive Psychology,* 1976, *8,* 561–577.

Minsky, M. "A Framework for Representing Knowledge." In P. H. Winston (Ed.), *The Psychology of Computer Vision.* New York: McGraw-Hill, 1975.

Nicholas, D. W., and Trabasso, T. "Goals, Themes, Inferences, and Memory." In F. Wilkening, J. Becker, and T. Trabasso (Eds.), *Information Integration by Children.* Hillsdale, N.J.: Erlbaum, 1980.

Pichert, J. W., and Anderson, R. C. "Taking Different Perspectives on a Story." *Journal of Educational Psychology,* 1977, *69,* 309–315.

Rumelhart, D. E. "Notes on a Schema for Stories." In D. C. Bobrow and A. M. Collins (Eds.), *Representation and Understanding: Studies in Cognitive Science.* New York: Academic Press, 1975.

Rumelhart, D. E. "Understanding and Summarizing Brief Stories." In D. La Berge and J. Samuels (Eds.), *Basic Processes in Reading: Perception and Comprehension.* Hillsdale, N.J.: Erlbaum, 1977.

Rumelhart, D. E., and Ortony, A. "The Representation of Knowledge in Memory." In R. C. Anderson, R. J. Spiro, and W. E. Montague (Eds.), *Schooling and the Acquisition of Knowledge.* Hillsdale, N.J.: Erlbaum, 1977.

Schank, R. C. "The Structure of Episodes in Memory." In D. G. Bobrow and A. M. Collins (Eds.), *Representation and Understanding: Studies in Cognitive Science.* New York: Academic Press, 1975.

Schank, R. C., and Abelson, R. P. *Scripts, Plans, Goals, and Understanding.* Hillsdale, N.J.: Erlbaum, 1977.

Snyder, M., and Uranowitz, S. W. "Reconstructing the Past: Some Cognitive Consequences of Person Perception." *Journal of Personality and Social Psychology,* 1978, *38,* 941–950.

Stein, N. L. "How Children Understand Stories." In L. Katz (Ed.), *Current Topics in Early Childhood Education.* Vol. 2. Norwood, N.J.: Ablex, 1979.

Stein, N. L., and Glenn, C. G. "An Analysis of Story Comprehension in Elementary School Children." In R. O. Freedle (Ed.), *New Directions in Discourse Processes.* Vol. 2: *Advances in Discourse Processes.* Hillsdale, N.J.: Erlbaum, 1979.

Stein, N. L., and Nezworski, T. "The Effects of Organization and Instructional Set of Story Memory." *Discourse Processes,* 1978, *1,* 177-193.

Stein, N. L., and Trabasso, T. "What's in a Story: An Approach to Comprehension and Instruction." In R. Glaser (Ed.), *Advances in the Psychology of Instruction.* Vol. 2. Hillsdale, N.J.: Erlbaum, in press.

Stein, N. L., Trabasso, T., and Garfin, D. "The Development of Inferential Thinking Skills: Comprehension of Moral Dilemmas." Paper presented at the convention of the American Psychological Association, New York, Sept. 1979.

Surbey, P. D. "Preschool Children's Understanding of Emotional States in Terms of Causes and Consequences." Unpublished master's thesis, University of Minnesota, 1979.

Thorndyke, P. W. "Cognitive Structures in Comprehension and Memory of Narrative Discourse." *Cognitive Psychology,* 1977, *9,* 77-110.

Trabasso, T. "On the Making of Inferences During Reading and Their Assessment." In J. T. Guthrie (Ed.), *Reading Comprehension and Teaching: Research Reviews.* Newark, Del.: International Reading Association, 1981.

Trabasso, T., Isen, A., Doleck, P., McLanahan, A., Riley, C. A., and Tucker, T. "How Do Children Solve Class-Inclusion Problems?" In R. Siegler (Ed.), *Children's Thinking: What Develops?* Hillsdale, N.J.: Erlbaum, 1978.

Trabasso, T., Stein, N. L., and Johnson, L. R. "Children's Knowledge of Events: A Causal Analysis of Story Structures." In G. Bower (Ed.), *Learning and Motivation.* Vol. 15. New York: Academic Press, in press.

Warren, W. H., Nicholas, D. W., and Trabasso, T. "Event Chains and Inferences in Understanding Narratives." In R. Freedle (Ed.), *New Directions in Discourse Processing.* Vol. 2. *Advances in Discourse Processes.* Hillsdale, N.J.: Erlbaum, 1979.

Wilensky, R. "Why John Married Mary: Understanding Stories Involving Recurring Goals." *Cognitive Science,* 1978, *2,* 235-266.

Wimmer, H. "Children's Understanding of Stories: Assimilation by a General Schema for Actions or Coordination of Temporal Relations?" In F. Wilkening, J. Becker, and T. Trabasso (Eds.), *Information Integration by Children.* Hillsdale, N.J: Erlbaum, 1980.

Tom Trabasso is professor of education and behavioral sciences at the University of Chicago. A cognitive psychologist, he studies how people, especially children, understand, reason, and remember language.

In our attempts to make sense of reality and to go beyond our immediate experience, we make a trade-off between consistency and inconsistency of response.

On the Surprise and Delight of Inconsistent Responses

Robin M. Hogarth

In a classic paper, Bruner (1957) captured a central theme of this volume when he wrote, "The most characteristic thing about mental life . . . is that one constantly goes beyond the information given" (p. 41). This is the process of practical inference, which chapters in this volume illustrate in the areas of judgment and choice (Slovic, Fischhoff, and Lichtenstein; Tversky and Kahneman), posing problems and questions (Getzels), using memory (Loftus), responding to questionnnaires (Bradburn), and understanding written and verbal communication (Trabasso). A further theme is that the responses generated in practical inference exhibit variability and are often inconsistent. Moreover, such inconsistency is generally deemed to be troublesome.

The law of requisite variety (Beer, 1966) states that to cope with a particular environment, a response system must have sufficient variety within it to match the degree of environmental variability. Thus, since variability characterizes the environments in which people make practical inferences, it is to be expected that human responses will also exhibit variability. Indeed, when people are placed in situations that lack external stimulation and thus environ-

I wish to thank Hillel J. Einhorn for many useful conversations during the preparation of this chapter. This preparation and the editing of this volume were facilitated by a grant from the Engineering Psychology Programs, Office of Naval Research.

R. Hogarth (Ed.). *New Directions for Methodology of Social and Behavioral Science: Question Framing and Response Consistency*, no. 11. San Francisco: Jossey-Bass, March 1982.

92

mental variability, they experience stress and generate their own variability by having thoughts, humming tunes, and so on (Fiske and Maddi, 1961). Physical perception also depends precisely on internally generated movement, and hence on variability, to generate images (Neisser, 1976; Platt, 1961). To demonstrate these points, readers are invited to fix on a blank sheet of paper and see how long they can look only at the paper and experience no variability of mental imagery or thoughts. This period is remarkably short.

Since variability of response is inherent in human inference, it is appropriate to ask how it affects this process and, in particular, to investigate its relationship to inconsistency. This is the goal of the present chapter, which is organized as follows: First, I discuss various meanings of inconsistency and how they are related to the concept of variability. I argue that consistency is a relative concept (consistency with what?) and that failure to recognize this has led to confusion in the literature. Second, I point out that practical inference can have many goals and that it consists of several stages or types of inference. Furthermore, the functionality of consistency and inconsistency varies both with the goals and with the types of inference that are considered. Third, since understanding and constructing hypotheses are vital to practical inference, I examine sources of consistency and inconsistency in these processes. Specifically, I argue that various cues used by the organism to establish order out of chaos can also limit the perception of alternative, fruitful interpretations of stimuli. This demonstrates the existence of a consistency-inconsistency trade-off that has important implications for mental activity. It is illustrated by aspects of the psychology of both humor and creativity.

Meanings of Consistency and Inconsistency

Consistency is a relative concept that has several meanings. From one perspective, consistency underlies normative systems that are used as guides to behavior (for example, arithmetic, deductive logic, probability theory, and so on). I refer to this as *logical* consistency. Its utility can be illustrated by the following anecdote about Bertrand Russell: "Russell is reputed at a dinner party once to have said, 'Oh, it is useless talking about inconsistent things, from an inconsistent proposition you can prove anything you like.' . . . . Somebody at the dinner table said, 'Oh, come on!' He said, 'Well, name an inconsistent proposition,' and the man said, 'Well, what shall we say, two equals one.' 'All right,' said Russell, 'what do you want me to prove?' The man said, 'I want you to prove that you are the pope.' 'Why,' said Russell, 'the pope and I are two, but two equals one, therefore, the pope and I are one.'" (Bronowski, 1978, pp. 78–79). Here, consistency refers to the manner in which logical principles are applied within particular inferential frameworks at a specific point in time. Furthermore, note that logical consistency has an all or nothing quality; conclusions are either consistent or inconsistent with premises.

From another perspective, consistency often refers to the regularity with which people apply behavioral rules in responding to given stimuli, as when making judgments. This I call *process* consistency, because it refers to consistency of behavioral processes across time, not to consistency with normative principles at one moment in time. Furthermore, whereas the former is a psychological phenomenon, the latter is a logical issue. An additional difference is that process consistency is not absolute, in that one can conceive of degrees of consistency.

Process consistency can itself also be considered from two viewpoints. One concerns the consistency with which a person responds to the same stimulus configuration on two independent occasions. The other concerns the consistency with which a person applies the same behavioral rule across a series of stimuli. In the first case, inconsistency is directly related to variability (consider test-retest correlations); however, this is not true in the second case, since the consistent application of a behavioral rule can lead to high variability across a series of stimuli. Imagine, for example, the outcomes that would result from consistent application of a disjunctive decision rule in choosing job candidates (Einhorn, 1970). Although the selected candidates can exhibit high variability on different attributes (such as levels of skill, motivation, prior experience), the rule that selected them was highly consistent. However, inconsistent use of behavioral rules is typically associated with high variability of responses; thus, the latter is often used as a cue to the former.

This example emphasizes the fact that although responses can be observed, underlying processes must be inferred. To illuminate this, consider how responses can be classified as outcomes of both logical and process consistency and inconsistency. Table 1 presents such a classification in a two-by-three format. The columns of Table 1 refer to consistency and inconsistency with logical principles and to irrelevance of logical principles, to account for instances where there are no such principles. The rows in Table 1 denote consistency and inconsistency with behavioral rules and processes. It must be emphasized that Table 1 is not comprehensive, but only a conceptual device to clarify this discussion. For example, a response could be classified as logically consistent by one normative scheme, but inconsistent by another. Furthermore, the classification

Table 1. Responses to Stimuli Classified by Consistency/Inconsistency with Behavioral Processes (Rows) and Logical Principles (Columns)

		Relative to Logical Principles		
		Consistent	Inconsistent	Irrelevant
Relative to Behavioral Processes/Rules	Consistent	1	2	3
	Inconsistent	4	5	6

of a behavioral rule could depend upon the level of analysis adopted. For example, if behavioral processes are hierarchical in nature (Simon, 1969), such that lower-level rules are selected for use by higher-level rules (or metaprocesses), what could appear to be inconsistent rule usage at one level could well be generated by consistent use of higher-level processes. For instance, Einhorn, Kleinmuntz, and Kleinmuntz (1979) have demonstrated that the fine-grained and apparently inconsistent cognitive processes revealed within the process-tracing methodology can be compatible with the simpler formulation of consistent linear decision rules.

First, consider responses in Table 1 that can be classified as consistent or inconsistent from the logical perspective (that is, cells 1, 2, 4, and 5). In two of these cells (1 and 5) the classifications are coherent, in the sense that both principles and processes classify responses as consistent or inconsistent. In contrast, cells 2 and 4 represent conflicts between the two criteria of consistency.

Cell 4 can be viewed from two perspectives. In one, the person uses a behavioral rule inconsistently but not so inconsistently that principles of logical consistency are violated. For example, fluctuations in attention produce random disturbances across a series of evaluative judgments but in a way that does not contradict normative principles, such as transitivity. This does not, however, imply that such inconsistencies are not dysfunctional; indeed, much judgmental activity is probably of this type (Goldberg, 1970).

In the other, people make responses by different processes, but observations are logically consistent and they may exhibit little or no variability. An example suggested by Tversky (1969) is the use of additive and additive difference models in the evaluation of multidimensional stimuli. Although these models can make identical choices that conform to normative principles, they represent different psychological processes. In one, each alternative is evaluated holistically and separately from others; in the other, alternatives are processed simultaneously by examination of differences between attributes.

As Tversky (1969) also illustrates, people are often unaware of the logical inconsistencies implied by their behavioral rules. However, there is an important difference in the awareness of such inconsistency when responses can be classified in cell 4, on the one hand, and in cell 2, on the other. In cell 4, logical inconsistency can often be resolved by noting that its origin lies either in variability in the use of a particular behavioral rule or in the application of different rules to the same stimulus configuration. Awareness of cell 2 responses, however, is invariably accompanied by both surprise and conflict. As examples, consider the reactions of Tversky and Kahneman's subjects when they respond inconsistently to the same problem framed in different ways. The surprise lies precisely in the recognition of the consistent (that is, the systematic) nature of the behavioral process that induces logically inconsistent responses. Conflict exists in that once inconsistency is recognized, people strive to reduce it. However, the conflict can only be resolved by denying either one's logical principles or one's behavioral rules. For instance, consider optical illusions, such as the Müller-Lyer. Here, the conflict between perceptual impressions and knowledge of physical measures is resolved by admitting that a ruler is more valid than one's eyes. In other cases, we may prefer intuition to a rule (for example, in choices that violate the principles of expected-utility theory; see the chapter by Tversky and Kahneman in this volume).

Whereas awareness of logical inconsistency is often accompanied by conflict, awareness of process inconsistency can produce delight. This happens with the realization that there can be multiple responses to the same stimulus, and it occurs in situations where there are no formal principles to which appeal can be made to determine the appropriate response (cell 6). In perception, this phenomenon is evidenced in reactions to reversible figures. It is also represented in reactions to the seemingly disparate domains of art, creative problem solving (see the chapter by Getzels in this volume), and humor. Indeed, Koestler (1964) has termed these the "Ah!", "Aha!", and "Haha!" reactions, respectively, noting that they all depend on recognizing alternative representations of the same stimulus. For example, consider the following story: "A woman at a formal dinner was quite discomfited to observe that the man across from her was piling his sliced carrots carefully upon his head. She watched with horror as the pile grew higher and higher and the sauce began to drip from his hair. She could finally stand it no longer, so she leaned toward him and said, 'Pardon me, sir, but why on earth are you piling your carrots on your head?' 'My God,' said he, 'are they carrots? I thought they were sweet potatoes'" (Adams, 1976, pp. 35–35).

Why do people find this and other, similar stories amusing? Although this volume has stressed the negative consequences of human sensitivity to the way in which questions and problems are asked and framed, could this same sensitivity not also have functional implications, for example, in seeing problems from new perspectives or in enjoying humor (Platt, 1961)?

Types of Inference

Human error has provided much insight into psychological processes. In the study of inference, logical inconsistencies have often assumed the role of error, even though one could debate what is or is not an error in specific circumstances. Evidence indicates that people judge inferential rules by their practical usefulness and thus do not always constrain themselves to the logical implications of formal systems. For example, the conclusions of syllogistic reasoning tend to be judged by the degree to which they match experience rather than by the legitimacy of logical operations (Henle, 1962). In other circumstances, logical errors are exactly implied. For instance, the statement "If you mow the lawn, I'll give you $5" carries with it the implication that the person will not receive the $5 unless he or she also mows the lawn (if p implies q, then not-p implies not-q, which is the error of denying the antecedent; Harris and Monaco, 1978).

These examples illustrate some differences between formal and practical inference. First, people differentiate between situations in which they believe that their behavior should be constrained by logical consistency and situations in which they do not. For instance, whereas most people would act on the logically incorrect conclusion that not mowing the lawn would imply not receiving the $5, few people would not wish to follow the rules of arithmetic when calculating change in a store. Second, it is a consequence of Gödel's theorem that any formal inferential system based on principles of logical consistency is limited in the domain of its application (Nagel and Newman, 1958).

Third, it is important to recognize that there are different types or stages of inference. One useful typology was originally proposed by Aristotle (Zellner, 1971), who distinguished three types: abduction (or reduction), whereby theories and hypotheses are generated from data and experience — this is the constructive aspect of inference, where "going beyond the information given" involves creating an understanding of the situation that the person faces (see the chapter by Trabasso in this volume); deduction, whereby implications are derived from the theories or situational understanding that the person creates — as when predictions are deduced from a model or hypothesis; and induction, whereby the predictive aspects of theories are tested against data. In Bayesian probabilistic inference, for example, this third type is modeled by the manner in which evidence affects the degree of belief that a person holds in a hypothesis.

Logical consistency is crucial in both the deductive and inductive stages of inference. Inconsistency can lead to absurd conclusions within deductive systems (recall the Russell story), and within inductive inference the paradigmatic case is the so-called Dutch book argument (Ramsey, 1926). That is, inconsistency in the assessment of probabilities can be exploited within a betting situation by arranging a series of bets such that the inconsistent assessor loses, whatever the outcome. In deductive and inductive inference, logical consistency permits one to go "beyond the information given" by exploiting the entailments of one's existing belief system or premises. In abductive inference, there are no such logical principles. Responses of this kind therefore fall in cells 3 and 6, and they can be discussed only in terms of process consistency. Furthermore, it is the abductive or constructive aspects of inference that have the greatest practical importance, since one can neither predict from nor have confidence in a hypothesis that does not exist.

The nature of humor illustrates both the functional and dysfunctional aspects of process consistency in abductive inference. Consider the story of the man piling food on his head, and note the roles of both process consistency and the different types of inference. The story involves use of situational cues and prior knowledge to structure understanding in a particular way; that is, it creates a specific figure-ground relation through abductive inference. In this case, the fact that a man is piling food on his head is sufficiently bizarre to make one feel that this is the behavior that needs to be explained (use of deductive inference in the form of a prediction derived from one's understanding or abduction of the situation). Also involved is subsequent realization that there is an alternative representation, that is, a different figure-ground relation (use of induction in that evidence shows one's previous representation to have been inappropriate, and abduction to recreate another understanding of the scene). Good jokes often have the quality of high congruence between situational cues and prior knowledge such that it is difficult at first to imagine an alternative representation. The power and delight of the punch line, however, lie in the force and speed with which an alternative representation is suggested (that is, the "Haha!" reaction). Without process inconsistency, it is unclear that one could perceive the essential incongruity underlying humor (McGhee, 1979).

Others have also stressed the significance of inconsistent behavioral processes. Noting the uncertain nature of inference, Brunswik (1952), for example, argued that we mitigate the effects of uncertainty by using cues and behavioral rules in interchangeable fashion in order to capitalize upon the redundancy of equivocal cue-cue and cue-criterion relations in the environment. However, although intersubstitution implies behavioral inconsistency, inconsistency increases validity over a series of responses relative to situations where reliance is placed on a single, imperfectly valid cue or response. That is, unless one can be sure that a particular cue is perfectly valid and thus selects the one response required by the stimulus, an inconsistent strategy is to be preferred (Fiske, 1961). In competitive environments, too, inconsistency in behavioral rules can be functional by increasing the difficulty that others have in predicting one's actions (Hogarth and Makridakis, 1981).

The limits of the preceding argument should also be realized. Life involves many inferential tasks that vary both in frequency and in importance. For frequently encountered tasks or subtasks, it is important to make consistent responses or sequences of responses. Consider, for example, the reactions that one learns to make in driving a car. These have been practiced so frequently that processing becomes habitual or automatic. Furthermore, the consistency achieved by this process is functional in terms of mental effort (one does not relearn to drive every day), and it can be relied upon when action must be taken quickly, as in emergencies.

Sources of Consistency in Abductive Inference

The variable demands of the environment require that we operate at varying levels of process consistency. In the case of abductive inference, the need for this can be illustrated by the following argument: The construction or abduction of a hypothesis from data can be conceptualized as the placement of those data in a particular configuration. To simplify matters for illustrative purposes, consider that each datum can be characterized on two dimensions: the distinctiveness with which it is perceived and the type of relation that it has with other data. In perceptual terms, distinctive data form figure against ground, and the relations between distinctive data form the pattern comprising the figure. Now, consider the number of arrangements (patterns or scenarios) that can be formed from k distinct items of data. First, denote each datum as belonging either to figure or ground (that is, as being distinctive or not). In this case, $m = \sum_{i=1}^{k} \binom{k}{i}$ distinct figure-ground relations are possible; for example, for $k = 4$, $m = 15$; for $k = 7$, $m = 127$; and for $k = 10$, $m = 1{,}023$. Second, conditional on any figure-ground relation, there are many ways in which the distinctive items of data can be arranged. For example, if distinctive data are characterized in pattern purely by time order, as in a story, the total number of ways in which i distinctive items could be arranged would be $i!$. Thus, considering only distinctive figure-ground combinations and different time order possibilities, the number of possible arrangements or scenarios of k items of data becomes $n = \sum_{i=1}^{k} \binom{k}{i} i!$; to illustrate, for $k = 4$, $n = 64$; for $k = 7$, $n = 13{,}699$; and for $k = 10$, $n = 9{,}864{,}100$.

The implication of this argument is that abduction is necessarily based on the inconsistent application of behavioral rules, whereby one arrangement is selected for differential treatment. That is, it would be impossible to establish order out of chaos without rules, but it would be impossible to achieve novel perspectives without inconsistency. Rules, however, imply regularity; thus, it is important to seek the higher-level principles by which the representation of a task is abduced in the form of both structure and specific content. Given the virtually infinite variability of environmental stimuli, I argue that structure is necessarily abduced through content (Einhorn and Hogarth, 1981a). Content, however, is dependent on meaning, and although the latter is an awkward, ill-defined concept, it requires elucidation.

One important function of meaning is to link and to keep previously distinct items of data, prior notions, and so on together. Indeed, many theorists argue that long-term memory is a reconstructive process and thus heavily dependent upon meaning. Furthermore, for a goal-oriented organism, linkages are likely to reflect the survival advantages of actions induced via inference, at least in the short run (Einhorn and Hogarth, 1981a; Lopes, 1981). These include accuracy of prediction, control of the environment through knowledge of causal relations, and invention to change the environment in one's favor. Moreover, although some predictions can be made without recourse to causal notions (that is, by simply noting co-occurrences—for example, that day follows night), causal understanding underlies much of this functional significance. Without claiming to provide a comprehensive account of abduction, the view taken here is that behavioral regularities implied by notions of causality are fundamental to this process.

The psychological meaning of cause has been discussed extensively elsewhere (Einhorn and Hogarth, 1981b). Here, I note three aspects relevant to this chapter. First, causal statements are framed within a context or specific causal field (Mackie, 1974; see also the chapter by Trabasso in this volume). The importance of the causal field is that it defines what the person regards as central and peripheral (that is, as figure or ground) in conceptualizing a given issue. For example, in the story about the man who piled food on his head, the man's unusual behavior was intrusive against the normal background of conduct at a dinner party, and so it became the figure in the ground of the lady diner. Shifts in the focus of attention, however, can change the nature of causal reasoning within the same objective situation. Thus, for the man in the story, piling food on his head was normal (that is, ground), and the figure was the fact that he was placing carrots and not sweet potatoes.

Second, causal thinking is highly dependent upon the elimination of alternative explanations through the use of counterfactual reasoning. Thus, in any given circumstances (that is, within a particular causal field), determining whether X is a cause of Y is done by asking questions of the form "Would X have occurred if Y had not?" Mackie (1974) illustrates this by contrasting the following two scenes: "(A) A chestnut is stationary on a flat stone. I swing a hammer down so that it strikes the chestnut directly from above. The chestnut becomes distinctly flatter than before. (B) A chestnut is stationary on a hot sheet of iron. I swing a hammer down so that it strikes the chestnut directly from above. At the very instant the hammer touches it, the chestnut explodes with a loud pop and its fragments are scattered around" (Mackie, 1974, p. 29). As Mackie goes on to say, "I assume that we now know or perceive enough about sequences A and B to be able to say that the chestnut's becoming flatter in A was caused by its being hit with the hammer, but that it's exploding in B was not caused by its being hit with the hammer" (p. 29).

Third, in determining the variables that may be relevant in a given situation, Einhorn and Hogarth (1981b) postulate that people use both prior causal notions and cues that direct attention to potentially relevant variables (called "cues to contingency and causality"). These cues are equivocal, but they do have ecological validity. However, since people cannot be certain of the validity of particular cues in specific circumstances, the cues are used in an interchangeable, inconsistent manner (Brunswik, 1952). Indeed, reliance on single cues can lead to serious inferential errors.

Einhorn and Hogarth identify the following cues: similarity or resemblance; contiguity in time and space; covariation; temporal order; manipulability; and robustness of relations between variables. To illustrate the use of these cues in abduction, consider similarity and temporal order.

Judgments of similarity can play both minor and major roles in judgments of causality. At one extreme, similarity can be a simple aid to classification and thus suggest an appropriate causal model for dealing with a particular situation. At the other, it can provide a model for an unfamiliar phenomenon, as in the use of analogy or metaphor (Chapanis, 1961; Ortony, 1979). In attempting to explain an unfamiliar phenomenon, a search is made for a phenomenon with similar features that is understood. Deductions from the latter are then extrapolated to the former. However, to illustrate the imperfect ecological validity of a single cue, consider how quite different images can be generated if one chooses different metaphors for the same object, such as *computer* and *muscle* for the brain.

Similarity in terms of common features is also often used to establish connections between variables. For example, similarity between economic or political events in different countries could be used to suggest a common cause; for example, unrest and Communist agitation. A further aspect of similarity in causal judgments is the notion that causes should resemble effects, if not in physical appearance than at least in magnitude. One does not, for example, expect large rewards for little effort. Noting, however, that such congruence can also lead to errors, Mill termed it a deeply rooted but erroneous belief that "not only reigned supreme in the ancient world, but still possesses almost undisputed dominion over many of the most cultivated minds" (Nisbett and Ross, 1980, p. 115). As an example, Nisbett and Ross (1980) cite a medical theory called the "doctrine of signatures," in which cures for diseases were thought to be marked by their resemblance to the symptom of the disease. Thus, a curative power against jaundice was attributed to a substance having a bright yellow color.

Since causes precede effects, noting the temporal order of events is an important cue to causality. In particular, knowledge of temporal order considerably reduces the causal interpretations that can be placed on data. For instance, consider the previous example of the number of scenarios that could be generated from k items of data. When temporal order is allowed to vary without constraint, the effect on the total number of scenarios is dramatic; for example, for $k = 7$, an unspecified temporal order increases the number of possible scenarios by a factor of more than 100, that is, from 127 to 13,699.

Practical Inference, Humor, and Creativity

Causal thinking within abductive inference facilitates the task of creating order out of chaos by reducing the number of possible interpretations of data. However, the cost of establishing order is that the probability of achieving alternative and possibly more fruitful interpretations is reduced. Such alternative viewpoints are frequently accompanied by what Bruner (1962) called the hallmark of a creative enterprise, namely *effective surprise,* and can be illuminated by considering aspects of both humor and creative reasoning.

Many scenarios in which jokes are embedded are rich in cues and meaning, and thus they already restrict interpretation in significant ways. Consider, for instance, time order of events or physical and temporal contiguity. Thus, for directing the attention of an audience to specific interpretations, key devices include highlighting cues that have ecological validity but are inappropriate in the circumstances, and shifts in the causal field. (Recall the dinner story.) Linked to this, the storyteller must also be aware of and use the audience's common prior world knowledge. Not only can this be used to provide a set for the audience, but it will indicate whether people will be likely to engage in different types of counterfactual reasoning as elements are added to a story across time. Indeed, the use of prior world knowledge through counterfactual reasoning and the adoption of specific causal fields illustrate a point realized by many humorists, namely that people from different cultures possess different senses of humor. (For an application of this principle to what is considered interesting in science, see Davis, 1971.) A further point concerns the deliberate manipulation of redundancy between cues to causality. Once the listener has formulated an initial hypothesis, it is important for this to be strengthened by redundant information, so that the possibility of generating alternative explanations is reduced. Moreover, to the extent that redundancy rules out alternative explanations, the surprise value of the punch line will be greater. Another form of humor provides people with few or no cues to a reasonable hypothesis and then shows how seemingly disparate information can in fact be explained easily. A good example of this is provided by Trabasso in this volume, when he indicates that a seemingly incomprehensible passage can be understood in the context of washing clothes.

According to Campbell (1960), the creative process depends upon random variation and selective retention of ideas. The cues to causality, however, explain precisely why random variation is so difficult. That is, the very mechanisms that facilitate understanding also prevent the generation of novel ideas and hypotheses that are consistent with observable data. Nonetheless, recognition of this situation can lead to ways of overcoming these difficulties. For example, although theories of creativity are not well developed, many guides to the process do suggest means of countering forces that limit different interpretations of stimuli (Hogarth, 1980). For instance, in brainstorming, people are requested specifically to refrain from counterfactual reasoning; in the synectics technique, extensive use is made of similarity by way of analogies and paradox to enjoin previously disconnected ideas. Another suggestion involves exercises to avoid letting one's thoughts become trapped within specific directions.

Consistency is important in inference. However, strict consistency with principles can be advocated only within closed, formal systems. Practical inference necessarily takes us beyond formal systems and our immediate experience. Some inconsistency with behavioral rules and principles is both inevitable and desirable.

References

Adams, J. L. *Conceptual Blockbusting: A Pleasurable Guide to Better Problem Solving.* San Francisco, Calif.: San Francisco Book Company, 1976.

Beer, S. *Decision and Control.* New York: Wiley, 1966.

Bronowski, J. *The Origins of Knowledge and Imagination.* New Haven, Conn.: Yale University Press, 1978.

Bruner, J. S. "Going Beyond the Information Given." In J. S. Bruner and others (Eds.), *Contemporary Approaches to Cognition.* Cambridge, Mass.: Harvard University Press, 1957.

Bruner, J. S. *On Knowing: Essays for the Left Hand.* Cambridge, Mass.: Belknap Press, 1962.

Brunswik, E. *The Conceptual Framework of Psychology.* Chicago: University of Chicago Press, 1952.

Campbell, D. T. "Blind Variation and Selective Retention in Creative Thought as in Other Knowledge Processes." *Psychological Review,* 1960, *67,* 380–400.

Chapanis, A. "Men, Machines, and Models." *American Psychologist,* 1961, *16,* 113–131.

Davis, M. "That's Interesting! Towards a Phenomenology of Sociology and a Sociology of Phenomenology." *Philosophy of Social Science,* 1971, *1,* 309–344.

Einhorn, H. J. "The Use of Nonlinear, Noncompensatory Models in Decision Making." *Psychological Bulletin,* 1970, *73,* 221–230.

Einhorn, H. J., and Hogarth, R. M. "Behavioral Decision Theory: Processes of Judgment and Choice." *Annual Review of Psychology,* 1981a, *32,* 53–88.

Einhorn, H. J., and Hogarth, R. M. "Uncertainty and Causality in Practical Inference." Working paper, Center for Decision Research, University of Chicago, 1981b.

Einhorn, H. J., Kleinmuntz, D. N., and Kleinmuntz, B. "Linear Regression and Process-Tracing Models of Judgment." *Psychological Review,* 1979, *86,* 465–485.

Fiske, D. W. "The Inherent Variability of Behavior." In D. W. Fiske and S. R. Maddi (Eds.), *Functions of Varied Experience.* Homewood, Ill.: Dorsey, 1961.

Fiske, D. W., and Maddi, S. R. *Functions of Varied Experience.* Homewood, Ill.: Dorsey, 1961.

Goldberg, L. R. "Man Versus Model of Man: A Rationale, Plus Some Evidence for a Method of Improving on Clinical Inferences." *Psychological Bulletin,* 1970, *73,* 422–432.

Harris, R. J., and Monaco, G. E. "Psychology of Pragmatic Implication: Information Processing Between the Lines." *Journal of Experimental Psychology: General,* 1978, *107,* 1–22.

Henle, M. "On the Relation Between Logic and Thinking." *Psychological Review,* 1962, *69,* 366–378.

Hogarth, R. M. *Judgement and Choice: The Psychology of Decision.* Chichester, England: Wiley, 1980.

Hogarth, R. M., and Makridakis, S. "The Value of Decision Making in a Complex Environment: An Experimental Approach." *Management Science,* 1981, *27,* 93–107.

Koestler, A. *The Act of Creation.* New York: Macmillan, 1964.

Lopes, L. L. "Decision Making in the Short Run." *Journal of Experimental Psychology: Human Learning and Memory,* 1981, *7,* 377–385.

Mackie, J. L. *The Cement of the Universe: A Study of Causation.* Oxford, England: Clarendon Press, 1974.

McGhee, P. E. *Humor: Its Origin and Development.* San Francisco, Calif.: W. H. Freeman, 1979.

Nagel, E., and Newman, J. R. *Gödel's Proof.* New York: New York University Press, 1958.

Neisser, U. *Cognition and Reality: Principles and Implications of Cognitive Psychology.* San Francisco, Calif.: W. H. Freeman, 1976.

Nisbett, R. E., and Ross, L. *Human Inference: Strategies and Shortcomings of Social Judgment.* Englewood Cliffs, N.J.: Prentice-Hall, 1980.

Ortony, A. "Beyond Literal Similarity." *Psychological Review,* 1979, *86,* 161–180.

Platt, J. R. "Beauty: Pattern and Change." In D. W. Fiske and S. R. Maddi (Eds.), *Functions of Varied Experience.* Homewood, Ill.: Dorsey, 1961.

Ramsey, F. P. "Truth and Probability." In H. E. Kyburg, Jr. and H. E. Smokler (Eds.), *Studies in Subjective Probability.* New York: Wiley, 1964. (Originally published 1926.)

Simon, H. A. *The Sciences of the Artificial.* Cambridge, Mass.: M.I.T. Press, 1969.

Tversky, A. "Intransitivity of Preferences." *Psychological Review,* 1969, *76,* 31–48.

Zellner, A. *An Introduction to Bayesian Inference in Econometrics.* New York: Wiley, 1971.

Robin M. Hogarth is associate professor of behavioral science in the Graduate School of Business, University of Chicago, where he works in the Center for Decision Research.

Index

A

Abelson, R. P., 80, 88
Acts, framing of, 8–9, 22–24
Adams, J. L., 95, 101
Adjustment, and anchoring, 30, 32–33
Administration, problem formulation in, 45–47
Ainslie, G., 17, 18
Allais, M., 10, 18
Allport-Vernon-Lindzey Study of Values, 43
American Marketing Association, 73, 75
Anchoring, and adjustment, 30, 32–33
Anderson, R. C., 79, 81, 87, 88
Aristotle, 96
Arlin, P. K., 45, 48
Art, problem posing in, 43–45
Art Institute of Chicago, School of the, 43–45

B

Barath, A., 61
Barofsky, I., 35, 36
Bartlett, F. C., 80, 83, 87
Beer, S., 91, 101
Belson, W. A., 68, 69, 75
Binet, A., 53, 56, 61
Black, J. B., 83, 84, 87
Bourne, L. E., 52, 62
Bower, G. H., 83, 84, 87
Bradburn, N. M., 1, 65–76, 91
Bradshaw, J. M., 61, 62
Bransford, J. D., 79, 80, 81, 87
Braunstein, M. L., 9, 19, 23n, 24, 36
British Columbia, University of, 4
Bronowski, J., 92, 101
Brown, J. S., 80, 88
Bruner, J. S., 91, 100, 102
Brunswik, E., 97, 99, 102
Buhler, K., 78, 88
Bunge, M., 42, 48
Burtt, H. E., 53, 54, 62

C

Cady, H. M., 54, 62
Camp, C. J., 61, 62

Campbell, D. T., 101, 102
Cannell, C. F., 61
Cantril, H., 74, 75
Cause, psychological meanings of, 98–99
Certainty effect, and framing of contingencies, 10–11, 12
Chapanis, A., 99, 102
Choices: difficulty of, 29–31; elimination of aspects model of, 29; and framing of decisions, 3–20; justification related to, 29–31; phases in making, 5; psychology of, 17; reversals of preference in, 4, 13, 16; risk-averse, 4, 5, 8–9, 11; risk taking, 5
Collins, A., 80, 88
Combs, B., 36
Compatibility, bias for, 33
Comprehension: activating context for, 78–79; context and, 77–89; models for, 79–81; and schemata, 82
Concreteness, and framing of acts, 22–24
Consistency: concepts of, 92–95; logical, 92, 93, 94, 95, 96; process, 93, 95, 96–97; sources of, 97–100. *See also* Inconsistency
Context: activating, 78–79; analysis of, 77–89; examples of, 77–78, 79, 80; and insurance decisions, 26–28; and models for comprehension, 79–81; and schemata effects, 81–85; summary of, 87; words and thought related to, 85–87
Contingencies, framing of, 10–13, 24–26
Cornell University, 68
Corrigan, B., 36
Crowder, R. G., 52, 62
Crum, R., 6, 13, 19
Czikszentmihalyi, M., 37n, 43, 44, 48

D

Dahl, A. D., 84, 88
Davis, M., 101, 102
De Bono, E., 39, 48
Decision frame, concept of, 3
Decision making, theories of, 5–8

Decision problem: concept of, 3; concurrent, 9–11, 22–24
Decisions: and evaluation of prospects, 5–8; and explicit information, 24; framing of, 3–20
Dewey, J., 39, 40, 48
Dilemmas, problems related to, 37–39
Dodd, D. H., 61, 62
Dohrenwend, B. A., 67–68, 75
Dolecki, P., 86, 89
Dominowski, R. L., 52, 62
Duncker, K., 40, 48

E

Einhorn, H. J., 17, 18, 29, 35, 91*n*, 93, 94, 98, 99, 102
Einstein, A., 37, 40, 48
Ellsberg, D., 7, 18
Elster, J., 17, 18
Eraker, S. A., 6, 13, 18
Expected-utility model: of decision making, 5, 7, 11; and insurance decisions, 26

F

Fee, J., 69, 76
Fellner, W., 7, 18
Fischhoff, B., 1, 12, 14, 16, 17, 18, 19, 21–36, 91
Fishburn, P. C., 5, 6, 13, 18
Fiske, D. W., 92, 97, 102
Framing: of acts, 8–9, 22–24; alternative, and perspective, 4, 16–17; analysis of, 3–20; background of, 3–5; of contingencies, 10–13; discussion of, 16–18; and gains and losses, 5, 13; of outcomes, 13–16, 26–28; phase of, 5; and protective action, 12, 24–26; and response mode, 28–33; in risk assessment, 21–36
Friedman, M., 26, 35

G

Gains and losses: in framing, 5, 13; and prospect theory, 6
Galanter, E., 6, 18
Galileo, G., 42
Gallup poll, 65–66, 70
Gambles: choices and selling prices in, 32–33; and concreteness, 22–24; and framing of outcomes, 13

Garfin, D., 85, 89
Gaskill, H. V., 54, 62
General Social Survey (GSS), 70, 73, 74
Getzels, J. W., 1, 37–49, 91, 95
Glenn, C. G., 80, 83, 85, 89
Goldberg, L. R., 94, 102
Graesser, A. C., 83, 88
Grether, D. M., 9, 19, 32, 35
Griver, S., 38, 48

H

Harris, R. J., 55, 60, 62, 95, 102
Harris survey, 74
Henle, M., 42, 49, 95, 102
Hershey, J. C., 14, 19, 27, 28, 35
Hogarth, R. M., 1–2, 17, 18, 29, 35, 84, 91–103
Huber, G. P., 30, 35
Humor: inference related to, 100–101; and process consistency, 95, 96–97
Hunt, B., 85, 88
Hunt, M., 85, 88
Hyman, H. H., 74, 76

I

Inconsistency: analysis of, 91–103; concepts of, 92–95; and types of inference, 95–97. *See also* Consistency
Infeld, L., 37, 48
Inferences: of abduction, 96, 97–100; cues to, 99–100; of deduction, 96; humor and creativity related to, 100–101; of induction, 96; types of, 95–97
Information processing: and questions, 52, 56–60, 61; and response mode, 28–33; in risk assessment, 21–36
Insurance: and framing of contingencies, 12–13; and framing of outcomes, 13–14, 26–28; and social norms, 28
Interrogation: analysis of, 51–63; current research on, 55–58; historical perspective on, 53–55; narrative or interrogatory technique in, 54–55; question effects in, 51–53; and theory of answering, 61. *See also* Questions
Isen, A., 86, 89

J

Johnson, E. M., 30, 35
Johnson, K. A., 53, 59–60, 62

Johnson, L. R., 82, 84, 88, 89
Johnson, M., 79, 80, 81, 87
Johnson, N. S., 80, 83, 85, 88
Judgments, anchoring and adjustment in, 30, 32–33
Justification, choice related to, 29–31

K

Kahneman, D., 1, 3–20, 21, 22, 24, 25, 26, 28, 35–36, 91, 94, 95
Kant, I., 58
Kintsch, W., 82, 88
Kleinmuntz, B., 94, 102
Kleinmuntz, D. N., 94, 102
Kochenberger, G. A., 6, 13, 18
Koestler, A., 95, 102
Krauss, E., 74, 76
Kunreuther, H. C., 13, 19, 27, 28, 36

L

Lachman, J. L., 61, 62
Lachman, R., 61, 62
Ladd, E. C., Jr., 74, 76
Larkin, K., 80, 88
Larsson, S., 11, 19
Laughhunn, D. J., 6, 13, 19
Laurent, A., 61, 62
League of Women Voters, 30
Lehnert, W. G., 61, 62
Libby, W. L., 40–41, 49
Lichtenstein, S., 1, 8, 9, 12, 14, 16, 17, 18, 19, 21–36, 91
Lieblich, A., 9, 19
Lieblich, I., 9, 19
Lipton, J. P., 54, 61, 62
Loftus, E. F., 1, 51–63, 85, 88, 91
Lopes, L. L., 98, 102
Losses. *See* Gains and losses
Luce, R. D., 28, 36
Lush, D. E., 54–55, 62

M

MacCrimmon, K. R., 11, 19
McDermott, D., 40, 49
McGaw, B., 79, 87
McGhee, P. E., 97, 102
McGlothlin, W. H., 13, 19
Mackie, J. L., 83, 88, 89, 102
McLanahan, A., 86, 89
MacNeil, B. J., 34, 36

McPherson, R. B., 37n
MacPhillamy, D. J., 33, 36
Maddi, S. R., 92, 102
Maier, N. R. F., 40, 49
Makridakis, S., 97, 102
Mandler, J. M., 80, 83, 85, 88
March, J. G., 17–18, 19
Markman, E., 86, 88
Marquis, K. H., 54, 62
Marshall, J. C., 54, 61, 62
Marston, W. W., 54, 62
Matisse, H., 42
Mazis, M., 35, 36
Memory, alteration of, and questions, 58–60
Minsky, M., 80, 88
Monaco, G. E., 60, 62, 102
Moore, H., 38, 40, 43, 49
Morgenstern, O., 5, 20
Morris, L., 35, 36
Murray, J., 71, 76
Muscio, B., 53–54, 62

N

Nagel, E., 96, 102
National Institute of Education, 77n
National Opinion Research Center (NORC), 65–66, 69
National Science Foundation, 21n, 51n
Neisser, U., 92, 102
Newcombe, F., 61, 62
Newman, J. R., 96, 102
Nezworski, T., 85, 89
Nicholas, D. W., 81, 83, 88, 89
Nisbett, R. E., 17, 19, 100, 102
Noelle-Neumann, E., 73, 76

O

Office of Naval Research, 3n, 91n
Oregon, University of, 25
Ortony, A., 82, 88, 99, 102
Oskamp, S., 54, 62
Outcomes: compound, 14; framing of, 13–16, 26–28; lability of, 14; and psychological accounting, 14–15; and reference points, 13

P

Palmer, J. C., 56, 57, 62, 85, 88
Pauker, S. G., 34, 36

Payne, J. W., 6, 9, 13, 19, 23n, 24, 36
Payne, S. L., 65, 71, 76
Perlmutter, M., 82, 88
Perspective, and alternative framing, 4, 16–17
Piaget, J., 45
Pichert, J. W., 81, 88
Platt, J. R., 92, 95, 102
Pliner, P., 6, 18
Plott, C. R., 9, 19, 32, 35
Polanyi, M., 42, 49
Pratt, J. W., 16, 19
Presser, S., 72, 74, 76
Problems: in administration, 45–47; analysis of, 37–49; in art, 43–45; caveats on, 47; concept of, 40; conclusions on, 47–48; created, 41–47; dilemmas related to, 37–39; discovered, 41; formulation of, 37; investigating, 42–47; and labeling, 86; presented, 41; process of finding, 38; types of, 40–41
Prospect theory: of decision making, 5–8, 11, 17; and gains and losses, 6; and insurance decisions, 26; and pseudocertainty, 24; and reference point, 27–28; value function in, 6–8, 13–14; weighting function in, 7
Protective action, and framing of contingencies, 12, 24–26
Pseudocertainty effect: in framing of contingencies, 11–12; and protective action, 24–25

Q

Questions: and alteration of memory, 58–60; answering, theory of, 61; and contextual meaning, 73–75; effects of, in interrogation, 51–53; elements in, and changed meaning, 70–75; expectation and implicative types of, 53; information integration in, 58–60; internal wording of, 70–72; and labeling, 86; logical and pragmatic implications in, 60; misleading information in, 56–58; positive or negative wording of, 71; pretesting, 68–69; and response categories, 72–73; standardized, 67–68, 69–70; subjective and objective types of, 53; wording and meaning of, 67–70; wording effects in, 65–76; wording of, 53, 55–57, 59–60, 65–66; words and thoughts related to, 85–87. See also Interrogation

R

Raiffa, H., 5, 19, 30, 36
Ramsey, F. P., 96, 102
Rationality: bounded, 17; concept of, 3, 17–18
Reitman, W. R., 39, 49
Response mode: framing and information processing related to, 28–33; in risk assessment, 21–36
Responses: categories of, and questions, 72–73; inconsistent, 91–103; and law of requisite variety, 91–92; and logical or process consistency, 93–94
Riley, C., 86, 89
Risk assessment: analysis of, 21–36; anchoring and adjustment in, 30, 32–33; and compatibility bias, 33; and concreteness, 22–24; and eliciting labile values, 34; implications for, 34–35; in insurance decisions, 26–28; justification and choice in, 29–31; and protective action, 24–26; and public awareness, 34–35
Robertson, L. S., 25, 36
Roentgen, W. C., 41
Ross, L., 17, 19, 100, 102
Rugg, D., 71, 76
Rumelhart, D. E., 80, 82, 83, 84, 88
Russell, B., 92

S

Sachs, L., 38
Savage, L. J., 5, 15, 19, 26, 35
Schank, R. C., 80, 88
Schemata: and comprehension, 82; effects of, at encoding and in retrieval, 81–82; and emotional reactions, 84; goal-action-outcome hierarchy and, 84–85; story structures as, 83–85
Schoemaker, P. J. H., 14, 19, 27, 28, 35, 36
Schuman, H., 72, 74, 76
Schwartz, D. M., 45, 49
Seat belts, and framing of contingencies, 25–26
Seibert, J., 86, 88
Self-control, and preferences, 16–17, 18
Sheatsley, P. B., 74, 76
Shifrin, H. M., 17, 18, 20
Simon, H. A., 17, 19, 94, 103
Slovic, P., 1, 8, 9, 12, 14, 16, 17, 19, 21–36, 91

Smilansky, J., 45, 49
Smith, T., 70–71, 74, 76
Snee, T. J., 54–55, 62
Snyder, M., 86, 88
Sox, H. C., 6, 13, 18
Stanford University, 4
Stein, G., 48
Stein, N. L., 80, 83, 84, 85, 89
Stengel, B., 84, 88
Strotz, R., 17, 18, 19
Sudman, S., 72–73, 75
Sunk-cost effect, and framing of outcomes, 14
Surbey, P. D., 84, 89
Surveys: question-wording effects in, 65–76; response differences in, 65–66

T

Thaler, R., 13, 14, 15, 16, 17, 18, 19–20
Thorndyke, P. W., 83, 89
Trabasso, T., 2, 77–89, 91, 96, 99
Tucker, T., 86, 89
Turner, C., 74, 76
Tversky, A., 1, 3–20, 21, 22, 24, 25, 26, 28, 29, 35–36, 91, 94, 95, 103

U

Uranowitz, S. W., 86, 88
Utility model. *See* Expected-utility model

V

Vaccination, and pseudocertainty, 24–25
Value function, in prospect theory, 6–8, 13–14
Values, eliciting, 34
van Dijk, T. A., 82, 88
von Neumann, J., 5, 20

W

Warren, W. H., 81, 89
Weichselbaum, R., 34, 36
Wertheimer, M., 37, 40, 44, 49
Whipple, G. M., 53, 62
Wilensky, R., 83, 84, 89
Williams, M. D., 61, 62
Wimmer, H., 85, 89
Wise, A., 16, 19

Z

Zanni, G., 56, 62
Zeckhauser, R., 16, 19
Zellner, A., 96, 103

H
61
.Q3
1982

Question framing and
  response consistency